£ 4-50

YOUR FAMILY PRAYER BOOK

Your Family Prayer Book
An Easy Way to Pray Together Every Day

Carmen Rojas

Servant Publications
Ann Arbor, Michigan

The Scripture quotations contained herein are from the
Revised Standard Version Bible, Catholic Edition,
copyright 1965 and 1966 by the Division of Christian
Education of the National Council of the Churches of
Christ in the USA, and are used by permission.

Published by Servant Publications
P.O. Box 8617
Ann Arbor, Michigan 48107

Cover design by Michael Andaloro

90 91 92 93 94   10 9 8 7 6 5 4 3 2 1

Printed in the United States of America
ISBN 0-89283-664-4

Library of Congress Cataloging-in-Publication Data

Rojas, Carmen.
    Your family prayer book : an easy way to pray
together every day / Carmen Rojas.
        p.   cm.
    ISBN 0-89283-664-4
    1. Family—Prayer-books and devotions—
English. 2. Catholic Church—Prayer-books and
devotions—English. I. Title.
BX2170.F3R64   1990
249—dc20   90-47390

CONTENTS

Introduction

THE ANDERSON FAMILY gathers in the living room after dinner to pray the Rosary. Jan, the oldest daughter, carefully places the statue of the Madonna and Child on the coffee table, while Mike, the oldest son, puts a large blue candle before the statue and lights it. Signalling the start of the Rosary, Mr. Anderson makes the Sign of the Cross; and as if on cue, everyone kneels—even Mom with a nursing infant in her arms.

This scene of the daily or weekly family Rosary is a fond memory for many adult Catholics raising families today—although their own pattern of family prayer may be quite different. Many Catholic families today read Scripture regularly, discuss it, and then take time for intercessions, with more of an emphasis on spontaneity in prayer. Whatever pattern a particular family may adopt, it is important to make prayer a regular part of family life.

Of course, our primary worship of God is in the liturgy of the Mass, when we gather to re-present the perfect and acceptable sacrifice of Jesus to the Father. But our prayer also needs to be expressed at home if our relationship with God, and our children's relationship with him, is going to blossom and grow.

A PRAYER BOOK THAT ADDRESSES
THE CHALLENGES OF FAMILY PRAYER

But figuring out *how* and *when* to pray consistently as a family is anything but simple for most Catholics today. Too often long work hours or busy schedules for Mom and Dad, extracurricular school activities for the kids, and a host of other concerns crowd out family prayer. There's also the frustrating issue of developing a simple pattern of prayer that is easy enough for young children to follow and yet spiritually satisfying for older children and parents. (Just try explaining the logic of the Liturgy of the Hours to a five-year-old sometime.)

Your Family Prayer Book is designed to help Catholic families address these kinds of challenges. It provides a very simple pattern of family prayer that can be used every day, seasonally, or just on special family occasions and feasts. The pattern provided can take as little as four or five minutes a day, or can easily be expanded into ten or even fifteen minutes of family devotions. The format is simple enough for toddlers to follow, and yet the spiritual themes developed are challenging enough to feed the spiritual life of adults and teenagers.

Each daily entry includes these elements:

- The Sign of the Cross;
- A short passage from the Psalms;
- A Glory Be;
- A short Scripture reading, usually from the New Testament;
- A simple response to the reading;
- Three short family intercessions with responses—one for the family, one for church and global concerns, and one for special intentions;
- The Lord's Prayer and a Hail Mary.

Following the church year, a four-week cycle of entries is provided for use during the thirty-three weeks of Ordinary Time; one-week cycles for the short seasons of Advent and Christmas; and two-week cycles for the longer Lent and Easter Seasons. Additional chapters provide entries for special feasts and family celebrations, such as the Solemnity of All Saints, the Solemnity of the Assumption of Mary into Heaven, baptisms, anniversaries, and birthdays.

The readings and intercessions for entries focus on the particular theme or concern appropriate for the season or day being celebrated. For example, under the heading of Family Celebrations, the entry for birthdays includes this reading from Psalm 139:

O Lord, you have searched me and known me! . . . For you did form my inward parts, you did knit me together in my mother's womb. I praise you, for you are fearful and wonderful. Wonderful are your works! vv. 1-14

The family intercessions for birthdays are:

Heavenly Father, we ask your special blessing on (name of birthday celebrant) this day, according to your abundant promises. We also pray that you would grant (name) long life, filled with the knowledge of your saving love.
Lord, hear our prayer.

Heavenly Father, we thank you and praise you for the precious gift of life, and especially eternal life in Jesus Christ. May all Christians cherish this great gift. *Lord, hear our prayer.*

Heavenly Father, we ask for a joyous birthday celebration, that through it, you would increase our love for one another.
Lord, hear our prayer.

THE BENEFITS OF USING THIS FAMILY PRAYER BOOK

The varied spiritual fare provided by these intercessions and Scripture readings will make this prayer book profitable for parents, teenagers, and young adult children—throughout the church year and family calendar, or just on special occasions. The simple format and short responses also make it possible for young children to follow along in prayer.

Further, the Sign of the Cross, Lord's Prayer, Hail Mary, and Glory Be are all recited at some point during each entry, giving parents an opportunity to teach young children these traditional prayers which comprise the Rosary. In fact, if this prayer book is used every day by families with small children, most children age three and up will have memorized these prayers within several months.

This prayer book is ideal for families that have only a short amount of time for prayer together since it only takes four to five minutes to complete the prayers in each entry. The prayers could be recited in the morning before family members leave for work and school. Or they could be recited in the evening, before or after dinner, or before bedtime.

For families that want to pray for more than four to five minutes a day, parents could consider presenting a short lesson based on the main Scripture passage for the day. This might entail Dad or Mom reading the passage beforehand and jotting down a few thoughts for the lesson.

Such families might also consider expanding the time of intercessions. For instance, after praying the first two intercessions that are provided for each day, family members could spend a longer period of time lifting up special intentions that relate to concerns at home, school, and work. The format is designed for this kind of expansion since the third intercessory prayer is usually for special intentions, which are to be provided by family members.

Finally, prayers for immediate and extended family members and a collection of traditional Catholic prayers are included in the appendices. The prayers for family members could be used for special family anniversaries and occasions, or in time of need for a particular family member. All families will probably want to draw upon the collection of traditional family prayers from time to time—especially when introducing new prayers and devotions to young children.

How ever you use this prayer book—every day or occasionally— my prayer is that it may draw you and your children closer to Christ and his church. May it help prepare you and your loved ones for a lifetime and an eternity of loving God.

—Carmen Rojas

Part One

Special Seasons and Ordinary Time

ONE

Advent Season

One Week of Daily Entries / 14

EDITOR'S NOTE: One week of daily entries has been provided for use throughout the four weeks of Advent. Some families may wish to select other Scripture readings for alternate weeks to provide more variety throughout the four-week cycle. Keep in mind that depending upon which day Christmas falls in a particular year, Advent can range from a full four weeks to three weeks and one day.

SUNDAY

OPENING PRAYER

In the name of the Father . . .

Make me to know your ways, O Lord; teach me your paths. Lead me in your truth, and teach me, for you are the God of my salvation; for you I wait all the day long. . . . Good and upright is the Lord; therefore he instructs sinners in the way. He leads the humble in what is right, and teaches the humble his way. **Ps 25:4-9**
Glory Be.

SCRIPTURE READING

There was a man sent from God, whose name was John. He came for testimony, to bear witness to the light, that all might believe through him. He was not the light, but came to bear witness to the light. The true light that enlightens every man was coming into the world. He was in the world, and the world was made through him, yet the world knew him not. He came to his own home, and his own people received him not. But to all who received him, who believed in his name, he gave power to become children of God.

Jn 1:6-12

Lord, may your Word be a lamp unto our feet,
And a light upon our path.

FAMILY INTERCESSIONS

Lord Jesus, we pray for our family members, that we might live in truth and righteousness and be a light to the world.
Lord, hear our prayer.

Lord Jesus, we pray that the church may spread its truth and light all over the world, especially in lands which are hostile to the gospel. *Lord, hear our prayer.*

Lord Jesus, we pray now for these special intentions: (name them). *Lord, hear our prayer.*

THE LORD'S PRAYER & A HAIL MARY

MONDAY

OPENING PRAYER

In the name of the Father . . .

Arise, O Lord; O God, lift up your hand; forget not the afflicted. . . . O Lord, you will hear the desire of the meek; you will strengthen their heart, you will incline your ear to do justice to the fatherless and the oppressed, so that man who is of the earth may strike terror no more. **Ps 10:12-18**
Glory Be.

SCRIPTURE READING

There shall come forth a shoot from the stump of Jesse, and a branch shall grow out of his roots. And the Spirit of the Lord shall rest upon him, the spirit of wisdom and understanding, the spirit of counsel and might, the spirit of knowledge and the fear of the Lord. . . . He shall not judge by what his eyes see, or decide by what his ears hear; but with righteousness he shall judge the poor, and decide with equity for the meek of the earth. **Is 11:1-4**

Lord, may your Word be a lamp unto our feet,
And a light upon our path.

FAMILY INTERCESSIONS

Lord Jesus, may our family be always open to your grace and see you even in the very small and ordinary circumstances of our lives. *Lord, hear our prayer.*

Lord Jesus, may your church be prepared and ready for your return. *Lord, hear our prayer.*

Lord Jesus, you are full of power and might. In accordance with your will, grant all our needs this day, especially: (name them). *Lord, hear our prayer.*

THE LORD'S PRAYER & A HAIL MARY

TUESDAY

OPENING PRAYER

In the name of the Father . . .

I call upon you, for you will answer me, O God; incline your ear to me, hear my words. Wondrously show your steadfast love, O savior of those who seek refuge from their adversaries at your right hand. Ps 17:6-7
Glory Be.

SCRIPTURE READING

Be patient, therefore, brethren, until the coming of the Lord. Behold, the farmer waits for the precious fruit of the earth, being patient over it until it receives the early and the late rain. You also be patient. Establish your hearts, for the coming of the Lord is at hand. Do not grumble, brethren, against one another, that you may not be judged; behold, the Judge is standing at the doors. Jas 5:7-9

Lord, may your Word be a lamp unto our feet,
And a light upon our path.

FAMILY INTERCESSIONS

Heavenly Father, we pray that we, as a family, may do only what pleases you and that we may always avoid sin and all occasions of sin. *Lord, hear our prayer.*

Heavenly Father, we pray for all the leaders in the church, for the Holy Father, Pope (name), for all bishops and priests, that they may never cease to prepare your people for the final coming of your Son. We also pray for all the leaders of our country, that they may be righteous, honest, and just in all they do.
Lord, hear our prayer.

Heavenly Father, in your wisdom grant us our special intentions: (name them). *Lord, hear our prayer.*

THE LORD'S PRAYER & A HAIL MARY

WEDNESDAY

OPENING PRAYER

In the name of the Father . . .

I will sing of your steadfast love, O Lord, forever; with my mouth I will proclaim your faithfulness to all generations. For your steadfast love was established forever, your faithfulness is firm as the heavens. You have said, "I have made a covenant with my chosen one, I have sworn to David my servant: 'I will establish your descendants forever, and build your throne for all generations.'"

Glory Be.   **Ps 89:1-4**

SCRIPTURE READING

And I heard every creature in heaven and on earth and under the earth and in the sea, and all therein, saying, "To him who sits upon the throne and to the Lamb be blessing and honor and glory and might forever and ever!" And the four living creatures said, "Amen!" and the elders fell down and worshiped. **Rv 5:13-14**

Lord, may your Word be a lamp unto our feet,
And a light upon our path.

FAMILY INTERCESSIONS

Lord Jesus, the key to the Father's kingdom, come to our family. Refresh us, Lord, and free us from all sin, sickness, and harm.
Lord, hear our prayer.

Lord Jesus, Son of David, have mercy on your people. Bring back to the fold all Christians who have gone astray. Lord Jesus, the way to the Father, visit our nation and lead to yourself all those who have not acknowledged you as Lord. *Lord, hear our prayer.*

Lord Jesus, our King, hear our particular needs: (name them).
Lord, hear our prayer.

THE LORD'S PRAYER & A HAIL MARY

THURSDAY

OPENING PRAYER

In the name of the Father . . .

O continue your steadfast love to those who know you, and your salvation to the upright of heart! Let not the foot of arrogance come upon me, nor the hand of the wicked drive me away.

Ps 36:10-11

Glory Be.

SCRIPTURE READING

"Come to me, all who labor and are heavy laden, and I will give you rest. Take my yoke upon you, and learn from me; for I am gentle and lowly in heart, and you will find rest for your souls. For my yoke is easy, and my burden is light." **Mt 11:28-30**

Lord, may your Word be a lamp unto our feet,
And a light upon our path.

FAMILY INTERCESSIONS

Loving Father, we ask for the gifts of joy and hope for our family and for all those we love. *Lord, hear our prayer.*

Heavenly Father, have mercy on all those who do not believe in you and for those who do not accept Jesus as your Son. Grant them repentance and conversion. We also pray for the many people in the world who have no one to care for their needs—the poor, the oppressed, the sick, and the dying; bring them your help and salvation. *Lord, hear our prayer.*

Father, hear our special intentions: (name them).
Lord, hear our prayer.

THE LORD'S PRAYER & A HAIL MARY

FRIDAY

OPENING PRAYER

In the name of the Father . . .

Our God comes, he does not keep silence, before him is a devouring fire, round about him a mighty tempest. He calls to the heavens above and to the earth, that he may judge his people: "Gather to me my faithful ones, who made a covenant with me by sacrifice!" The heavens declare his righteousness, for God himself is judge! Ps 50:3-6
Glory Be.

SCRIPTURE READING

Behold, the Lord God comes with might, and his arm rules for him; behold, his reward is with him, and his recompense before him. He will feed his flock like a shepherd, he will gather the lambs in his arms, he will carry them in his bosom, and gently lead those that are with young. Is 40:10-11

Lord, may your Word be a lamp unto our feet,
And a light upon our path.

FAMILY INTERCESSIONS

God our Father, protect our family and provide us with all that we need to love and serve you. We ask this through Jesus, who is our Good Shepherd. *Lord, hear our prayer.*

Heavenly Father, we pray for all Christians, that they may be truly united in the love of Christ. Father, guide all the nations in the world, that they may seek to promote peace instead of war, and that they may find the solutions to their problems in Jesus Christ. *Lord, hear our prayer.*

Father, grant the special intentions we place before you: (name them). *Lord, hear our prayer.*

THE LORD'S PRAYER & A HAIL MARY

SATURDAY

OPENING PRAYER

In the name of the Father . . .

I will tell of the decree of the Lord: He said to me, "You are my son, today I have begotten you. Ask of me, and I will make the nations your heritage, and the ends of the earth your possession." **Ps 2:7-8** *Glory Be.*

SCRIPTURE READING

Arise, O Jerusalem, stand upon the height and look toward the east, and see your children gathered from west and east, at the Word of the Holy One, rejoicing that God has remembered them. For they went forth from you on foot, led away by their enemies; but God will bring them back to you, carried in glory, as on a royal throne. For God has ordered that every high mountain and the everlasting hills be made low and the valleys be filled up, to make level ground, so that Israel may walk safely in the glory of God. **Bar 5:5-7**

Lord, may your Word be a lamp unto our feet,
And a light upon our path.

FAMILY INTERCESSIONS

Lord Jesus, we pray that our family life would be a witness of your love and a light of truth to our neighbors and friends.
Lord, hear our prayer.

Lord Jesus, grant that every ruler and power may know you as the true Lord of the earth. Grant that the church may always be a powerful sign of your presence in the world. Grant that all Christian people may experience a true spiritual renewal and may have more zeal for their heavenly home. *Lord, hear our prayer.*

Lord Jesus, we entrust all of our other needs to you, and specifically pray for: (name them). *Lord, hear our prayer.*

THE LORD'S PRAYER & A HAIL MARY

Christmas Season

EDITOR'S NOTE: First, daily entries have not been provided for all the days of the Christmas Season, but only for the first week and special feasts of the church universal. Those who want to use this prayer book throughout the entire Christmas Season could repeat the entries provided for December 29 through December 31 during the second week of the season. Second, Epiphany is traditionally viewed as the last day of the Christmas Season. But since Epiphany is no longer celebrated on the fixed date of January 6 in the United States—the last of the traditional twelve days of Christmas—there are varying opinions about what should constitute the exact length of the season from year to year. For simplicity's sake, we recommend that families consider the Solemnity of Epiphany the last day of the season and turn to the section provided for Ordinary Time thereafter.

CHRISTMAS DAY
DECEMBER 25

OPENING PRAYER

In the name of the Father . . .

O sing to the Lord a new song, for he has done marvelous things! His right hand and his holy arm have gotten him victory. The Lord has made known his victory, he has revealed his vindication in the sight of the nations. He has remembered his steadfast love and faithfulness to the house of Israel. All the ends of the earth have seen the victory of our God. **Ps 98:1-3**
Glory Be.

SCRIPTURE READING

In many and various ways God spoke of old to our fathers by the prophets; but in these last days he has spoken to us by a Son, whom he appointed the heir of all things, through whom also he created the world. He reflects the glory of God and bears the very stamp of his nature, upholding the universe by his word of power. **Heb 1:1-3a**

Lord, may your Word be a lamp unto our feet,
And a light upon our path.

FAMILY INTERCESSIONS

Heavenly Father, as we celebrate the mystery of the incarnation this day, may our family become more grateful to you for the gift of your Son Jesus. *Lord, hear our prayer.*

Lord Jesus Christ, you are the Son of God, Emmanuel, God who is with us. May all Christians come to know you better and to worship you in all of your glory and majesty. *Lord, hear our prayer.*

Lord Jesus, Savior of the world, answer our special intercessions: (name them). *Lord, hear our prayer.*

THE LORD'S PRAYER & A HAIL MARY

FEAST OF ST. STEPHEN
DECEMBER 26

OPENING PRAYER

In the name of the Father . . .

You are my rock and my fortress; for your name's sake lead me and guide me, take me out of the net which is hidden for me, for you are my refuge. Into your hand I commit my spirit; you have redeemed me, O Lord, faithful God. Ps 31:3-5
Glory Be.

SCRIPTURE READING

Stephen, full of the Holy Spirit, gazed into heaven and saw the glory of God, and Jesus standing at the right hand of God; and he said, "Behold, I see the heavens opened, and the Son of man standing at the right hand of God." But they cried out with a loud voice and stopped their ears and rushed together upon him. . . . And as they were stoning Stephen, he prayed, "Lord Jesus, receive my spirit." And he knelt down and cried with a loud voice, "Lord, do not hold this sin against them." And when he had said this, he fell asleep. Acts 7:55-60

Lord, may your Word be a lamp unto our feet,
And a light upon our path.

FAMILY INTERCESSIONS

Father, help us and all Christians always to be faithful to Jesus and to express our faith without shame or fear. *Lord, hear our prayer.*

Father, we pray that all Christians, like St. Stephen, may love and forgive their enemies, and have the courage to bear the difficulties and trials in their lives. *Lord, hear our prayer.*

Loving Father, now hear our personal intentions: (name them).
Lord, hear our prayer.

THE LORD'S PRAYER & A HAIL MARY

FEAST OF ST. JOHN THE APOSTLE AND EVANGELIST
DECEMBER 27

OPENING PRAYER

In the name of the Father . . .

Oh, how I love your law! It is my meditation all the day. Your commandment makes me wiser than my enemies, for it is ever with me. I have more understanding than all my teachers, for your testimonies are my meditation. I understand more than the aged, for I keep your precepts. **Ps 119:97-100**
Glory Be.

SCRIPTURE READING

That which was from the beginning, which we have heard, which we have seen with our eyes, which we have looked upon and touched with our hands, concerning the word of life—the life was made manifest, and we saw it, and testify to it, and proclaim to you the eternal life which was with the Father and was made manifest to us—. . . **1 Jn 1:1-2**

Lord, may your Word be a lamp unto our feet,
And a light upon our path.

FAMILY INTERCESSIONS

Father, we thank you for the unity and fellowship we enjoy in Jesus as a family. Draw us ever closer together in your Son's steadfast love. *Lord, hear our prayer.*

Father in heaven, bless the Catholic church all over the world, that she may grow in zeal in bringing Christ to all the nations.
Lord, hear our prayer.

Father God, hear our special intentions for this day: (name them). *Lord, hear our prayer.*

THE LORD'S PRAYER & A HAIL MARY

FEAST OF THE HOLY INNOCENTS
DECEMBER 28

OPENING PRAYER

In the name of the Father . . .

If it had not been the Lord who was on our side, when men rose up against us, then they would have swallowed us up alive, when their anger was kindled against us; then the flood would have swept us away, the torrent would have gone over us. . . . Our help is in the name of the Lord, who made heaven and earth. **Ps 124:2-8** *Glory Be.*

SCRIPTURE READING

Then Herod, when he saw that he had been tricked by the wise men, was in a furious rage, and he sent and killed all the male children in Bethlehem and in all that region who were two years old or under, according to the time which he had ascertained from the wise men. **Mt 2:16**

Lord, may your Word be a lamp unto our feet,
And a light upon our path.

FAMILY INTERCESSIONS

Father, we ask for your grace and protection over the children in our family (name them). Keep them from all physical and spiritual harm. *Lord, hear our prayer.*

Father God, we pray for all children whose lives are threatened by famine, poverty, and want. Heavenly Father, also protect all unborn children from harm and danger, especially the threat of abortion. *Lord, hear our prayer.*

Heavenly Father, hear our special intentions: (name them).
Lord, hear our prayer.

THE LORD'S PRAYER & A HAIL MARY

DECEMBER 29

OPENING PRAYER

In the name of the Father . . .

O sing to the Lord a new song; sing to the Lord, all the earth! Sing to the Lord, bless his name; tell of his salvation from day to day. Declare his glory among the nations, his marvelous works among all the peoples! For great is the Lord, and greatly to be praised; he is to be feared above all gods. **Ps 96:1-4**
Glory Be.

SCRIPTURE READING

Now there was a man in Jerusalem, whose name was Simeon, and this man was righteous and devout, looking for the consolation of Israel, and the Holy Spirit was upon him. And it had been revealed to him by the Holy Spirit that he should not see death before he had seen the Lord's Christ. And inspired by the Spirit he came into the temple; and when the parents brought in the child Jesus, to do for him according to the custom of the law, he took him up in his arms and blessed God. **Lk 2:25-28**

Lord, may your Word be a lamp unto our feet,
And a light upon our path.

FAMILY INTERCESSIONS

Father, help us as parents to have the obedience and strength to do what you require of us in raising up our children to love and serve you. *Lord, hear our prayer.*

Father, may all Christians seek the Lord Jesus Christ and rejoice at his coming, like Simeon in the temple at the presentation of the infant Jesus. *Lord, hear our prayer.*

Lord, we especially pray for: (name them). *Lord, hear our prayer.*

THE LORD'S PRAYER & A HAIL MARY

PASSION SUNDAY

OPENING PRAYER

In the name of the Father . . .

My God, my God, why have you forsaken me? Why are you so far from helping me, from the words of my groaning? . . . A company of evildoers encircle me; they have pierced my hands and feet—I can count all my bones—they stare and gloat over me; they divide my garments among them, and for my raiment they cast lots.

Glory Be.

Ps 22:1-18

SCRIPTURE READING

And those who passed by derided him, wagging their heads, and saying, "Aha! You who would destroy the temple and build it in three days, save yourself, and come down from the cross!" So also the chief priests mocked him to one another with the scribes, saying, "He saved others; he cannot save himself. Let the Christ, the King of Israel, come down now from the cross, that we may see and believe." Mk 15:29-32

Lord, may your Word be a lamp unto our feet,
And a light upon our path.

FAMILY INTERCESSIONS

Lord Jesus Christ, we hail you as the crucified Lord and Savior of our family. Grant us throughout Holy Week a deeper appreciation of your passion and death. *Lord, hear our prayer.*

Lord Jesus Christ, we pray for those in need of salvation, that they may come to know you as Lord and Savior. We pray for the church all over the world, that she may be renewed and strengthened by God. *Lord, hear our prayer.*

Lord Jesus Christ, grant our special needs as a family: (name them). *Lord, hear our prayer.*

THE LORD'S PRAYER & A HAIL MARY

HOLY THURSDAY

OPENING PRAYER

In the name of the Father . . .

What shall I render to the Lord for all his bounty to me? I will lift up the cup of salvation and call on the name of the Lord, I will pay my vows to the Lord in the presence of all his people. Ps 116:12-14
Glory Be.

SCRIPTURE READING

For I received from the Lord what I also delivered to you, that the Lord Jesus on the night when he was betrayed took bread, and when he had given thanks, he broke it, and said, "This is my body which is for you. Do this in remembrance of me." In the same way also the cup, after supper, saying, "This cup is the new covenant in my blood. Do this, as often as you drink it, in remembrance of me." 1 Cor 11:23-25

Lord, may your Word be a lamp unto our feet,
And a light upon our path.

FAMILY INTERCESSIONS

Lord Jesus, we thank you for the great gift of the Eucharist, your body and blood, given to be our spiritual food. Grant that we as a family may enter more fully into the mystery of your passion and death. *Lord, hear our prayer.*

Lord Jesus, we pray for the renewal and unity of all Christians in the world, that we might be one as you and the Father are one. *Lord, hear our prayer.*

Lord Jesus, we pray for our friends and relatives who need prayer: (name them). *Lord, hear our prayer.*

THE LORD'S PRAYER & A HAIL MARY

GOOD FRIDAY

OPENING PRAYER

In the name of the Father . . .

In you, O Lord, do I seek refuge; let me never be put to shame; in your righteousness deliver me! Incline your ear to me, rescue me speedily! Be a rock of refuge for me, a strong fortress to save me! Into your hand I commit my spirit; you have redeemed me, O Lord, faithful God. Ps 31:1-5
Glory Be.

SCRIPTURE READING

Surely he has borne our griefs and carried our sorrows; yet we esteemed him stricken, smitten by God, and afflicted. But he was wounded for our transgressions, he was bruised for our iniquities; upon him was the chastisement that made us whole, and with his stripes we are healed. Is 53:4-5

Lord, may your Word be a lamp unto our feet,
And a light upon our path.

FAMILY INTERCESSIONS

Lord Jesus, help each member of our family to draw near to you. May each of us pick up our cross daily and follow you. Help us to totally surrender ourselves to you, to trust you fully with our lives. *Lord, hear our prayer.*

Lord Jesus, we pray for the whole church, especially our Holy Father, Pope (name), and our bishop, (name), along with all the faithful. May all of us be inspired by your death and passion. *Lord, hear our prayer.*

Lord Jesus, hear our special intentions for those we know who do not know you: (name them). *Lord, hear our prayer.*

THE LORD'S PRAYER & A HAIL MARY
(see Appendix for a modified Family Way of the Cross.)

FOUR

Easter Season

EDITOR'S NOTE: This chapter includes a two-week cycle of daily entries for use throughout the seven weeks of the Easter Season and provides entries as well for Easter Sunday, Ascension Thursday, and Pentecost. The Easter Season is fifty days long, starting on Easter Sunday and ending on Pentecost Sunday. At the end of the Easter Season, families should return to the four-week cycle provided for Ordinary Time.

EASTER SUNDAY

OPENING PRAYER

In the name of the Father . . .

Hark, glad songs of victory in the tents of the righteous: "The right hand of the Lord does valiantly, the right hand of the Lord is exalted!" I shall not die, but I shall live, and recount the deeds of the Lord. The Lord has chastened me sorely, but he has not given me over to death. **Ps 18:15-18**
Glory Be.

SCRIPTURE READING

And very early on the first day of the week they went to the tomb when the sun had risen. . . . And entering the tomb, they saw a young man sitting on the right side, dressed in a white robe; and they were amazed. And he said to them, "Do not be amazed; you seek Jesus of Nazareth, who was crucified. He has risen, he is not here; see the place where they laid him. But go, tell his disciples and Peter that he is going before you to Galilee; there you will see him, as he told you." **Mk 16:2-7**

Lord, may your Word be a lamp unto our feet,
And a light upon our path.

FAMILY INTERCESSIONS

Come, Lord Jesus Christ, and fill us, as a family, with the joy of your resurrection, that we may go and tell the good news.
Lord, hear our prayer.

Come, Lord Jesus Christ, and help your church to experience victory over sin and death, that we may all rise to new life.
Lord, hear our prayer.

Come, Lord Jesus Christ, and lead us to the gates of heaven. We especially pray for our deceased loved ones: (name them).
Lord, hear our prayer.

THE LORD'S PRAYER & A HAIL MARY

SUNDAY
WEEK ONE

OPENING PRAYER

In the name of the Father . . .

Answer me when I call, O God of my right! You have given me room when I was in distress. Be gracious to me, and hear my prayer . . . . Know that the Lord has set apart the godly for himself; the Lord hears when I call to him. . . . In peace I will both lie down and sleep; for you alone, O Lord, make me dwell in safety. **Ps 4:1-8**
Glory Be.

SCRIPTURE READING

"Let not your hearts be troubled; believe in God, believe also in me. In my Father's house are many rooms; if it were not so, would I have told you that I go to prepare a place for you? And when I go and prepare a place for you, I will come again and will take you to myself, that where I am you may be also." **Jn 14:1-3**

Lord, may your Word be a lamp unto our feet,
And a light upon our path.

FAMILY INTERCESSIONS

Risen Lord, we pray for greater faith in your work in the difficult circumstances of our family life and for eyes of faith to see your answers. *Lord, hear our prayer.*

Risen Lord, our faith is strengthened as we see you answer our prayers. We come before you this day to seek a renewal of faith among your people. We pray for all those who don't yet believe in you, that they would come to know your great love and care for them. *Lord, hear our prayer.*

Risen Lord, hear our special intentions: (name them).
Lord, hear our prayer.

THE LORD'S PRAYER & A HAIL MARY

MONDAY
WEEK ONE

OPENING PRAYER

In the name of the Father . . .

I keep the Lord always before me; because he is at my right hand, I shall not be moved. Therefore my heart is glad, and my soul rejoices; my body also dwells secure. For you do not give me up to Sheol, or let your godly one see the Pit. **Ps 16:8-10**
Glory Be.

SCRIPTURE READING

"Jesus of Nazareth, a man attested to you by God with mighty works and wonders and signs which God did through him in your midst, as you yourselves know—this Jesus, delivered up according to the definite plan and foreknowledge of God, you crucified and killed by the hands of lawless men. But God raised him up, having loosed the pangs of death, because it was not possible for him to be held by it." **Acts 2:22-24**

Lord, may your Word be a lamp unto our feet,
And a light upon our path.

FAMILY INTERCESSIONS

Risen Lord, we pray that each member of our family may say "no" to temptation and sin. Help us to know the pure joy of loving you. *Lord, hear our prayer.*

Risen Lord, we pray for all those who are in bondage to alcohol, drugs, and other addictions, that you may give them power to live in the freedom of your resurrection. *Lord, hear our prayer.*

Risen Lord, hear our special needs this day: (name them).
Lord, hear our prayer.

THE LORD'S PRAYER & A HAIL MARY

TUESDAY
WEEK ONE

OPENING PRAYER

In the name of the Father . . .

Praise the Lord! Praise God in his sanctuary; praise him in his mighty firmament! Praise him for his mighty deeds; praise him according to his exceeding greatness! Praise him with trumpet sound; praise him with lute and harp! . . . Let everything that breathes praise the Lord! **Ps 150**
Glory Be.

SCRIPTURE READING

And the high priest questioned them, saying, "We strictly charged you not to teach in this name, yet here you have filled Jerusalem with your teaching and you intend to bring this man's blood upon us." But Peter and the apostles answered, "We must obey God rather than men. The God of our fathers raised Jesus whom you killed by hanging him on a tree. God exalted him at his right hand as Leader and Savior, to give repentance to Israel and forgiveness of sins." **Acts 5:27-31**

Lord, may your Word be a lamp unto our feet,
And a light upon our path.

FAMILY INTERCESSIONS

Risen Lord, we ask for greater joy in our family life and in one another during this Easter season. *Lord, hear our prayer.*

Risen Lord, we pray for all those who are sorrowing or grieving, that God our Father may grant them his joy. Help all Christians to find joy in God rather than in earthly things. *Lord, hear our prayer.*

Risen Lord, we ask for our special needs: (name them).
Lord, hear our prayer.

THE LORD'S PRAYER & A HAIL MARY

WEDNESDAY
WEEK ONE

OPENING PRAYER

In the name of the Father . . .

Those who trust in the Lord are like Mount Zion, which cannot be moved, but abides for ever. As the mountains are round about Jerusalem, so the Lord is round about his people, from this time forth and for evermore.... Do good, O Lord, to those who are good, and to those who are upright in their hearts! **Ps 125:1-4**
Glory Be.

SCRIPTURE READING

For God so loved the world that he gave his only Son, that whoever believes in him should not perish but have eternal life. For God sent the Son into the world, not to condemn the world, but that the world might be saved through him. He who believes in him is not condemned; he who does not believe is condemned already, because he has not believed in the name of the only Son of God.

Jn 3:16-18

Lord, may your Word be a lamp unto our feet,
And a light upon our path.

FAMILY INTERCESSIONS

Risen Lord, we pray for the salvation of each member of our family. May each of us persevere in following you until we behold your glory in heaven. *Lord, hear our prayer.*

Risen Lord, we pray for all agnostics and atheists, that they would recognize your Father's hand in creation and come to a saving knowledge of you. *Lord, hear our prayer.*

Risen Lord, remember our special intentions of the day: (name them). *Lord, hear our prayer.*

THE LORD'S PRAYER & A HAIL MARY

THURSDAY
WEEK ONE

OPENING PRAYER

In the name of the Father . . .

Behold, how good and pleasant it is when brothers dwell in unity! It is like the precious oil upon the head, running down upon the beard, upon the beard of Aaron, running down on the collar of his robes! It is like the dew of Hermon, which falls on the mountains of Zion! For there the Lord has commanded the blessing, life for evermore. **Ps 133**
Glory Be.

SCRIPTURE READING

Now the company of those who believed were of one heart and soul, and no one said that any of the things which he possessed was his own, but they had everything in common. And with great power the apostles gave their testimony to the resurrection of the Lord Jesus, and great grace was upon them all. There was not a needy person among them, for as many as were possessors of lands or houses sold them, and brought the proceeds of what was sold and laid it at the apostles' feet; . . . **Acts 4:32-35**

Lord, may your Word be a lamp unto our feet,
And a light upon our path.

FAMILY INTERCESSIONS

Risen Lord, we pray for unselfishness and unity in our family.
Lord, hear our prayer.

Risen Lord, we pray for the unity of all Christians, especially for the unity of all those in our parish community.
Lord, hear our prayer.

Lord Jesus, we pray for our special needs: (name them).
Lord, hear our prayer.

THE LORD'S PRAYER & A HAIL MARY

FRIDAY
WEEK ONE

OPENING PRAYER

In the name of the Father . . .

The Lord brings the counsel of the nations to nought; he frustrates the plans of the peoples. The counsel of the Lord stands forever, the thoughts of his heart to all generations. Blessed is the nation whose God is the Lord, the people whom he has chosen as his heritage! Ps 33:10-12
Glory Be.

SCRIPTURE READING

It is to fulfill the word that is written in their law, "They hated me without a cause." But when the Counselor comes, whom I shall send to you from the Father, even the Spirit of truth, who proceeds from the Father, he will bear witness to me; and you also are witnesses, because you have been with me from the beginning.

Jn 15:25-27

Lord, may your Word be a lamp unto our feet,
And a light upon our path.

FAMILY INTERCESSIONS

Holy Spirit, let our family effectively witness to those who do not know Jesus. Make us bold and courageous in speaking about Jesus to people in our neighborhood, work, and school.
Lord, hear our prayer.

Holy Spirit, guide the work of all Christian missionaries to success. *Lord, hear our prayer.*

Holy Spirit, we pray for all our other intentions this day: (name them). *Lord, hear our prayer.*

THE LORD'S PRAYER & A HAIL MARY

SATURDAY
WEEK ONE

OPENING PRAYER

In the name of the Father . . .

These all look to you, to give them their food in due season. When you give to them, they gather it up; when you open your hand, they are filled with good things. When you hide your face, they are dismayed; when you take away their breath, they die and return to their dust. When you send forth your Spirit, they are created; and you renew the face of the ground. **Ps 104:27-30**
Glory Be.

SCRIPTURE READING

"If you love me, you will keep my commandments. And I will pray the Father, and he will give you another Counselor, to be with you forever, even the Spirit of truth, whom the world cannot receive, because it neither sees him nor knows him; you know him, for he dwells with you, and will be in you." **Jn 14:15-17**

Lord, may your Word be a lamp unto our feet,
And a light upon our path.

FAMILY INTERCESSIONS

Risen Lord, we pray for a fresh outpouring of the Holy Spirit upon our family that we would come to know you in a deeper way as our Savior. *Lord, hear our prayer.*

Risen Lord, we pray for the whole church, that the Holy Spirit would bring us to deeper conversion and unity with one another, so that the world may believe. We pray especially for the spiritual life of our parish, that we would be renewed and refreshed in the power of the Holy Spirit. *Lord, hear our prayer.*

Risen Lord, remember our special intentions: (name them).
Lord, hear our prayer.

THE LORD'S PRAYER & A HAIL MARY

SUNDAY
WEEK TWO

OPENING PRAYER

In the name of the Father . . .

When I look at your heavens, the work of your fingers, the moon and the stars which you have established; what is man that you are mindful of him, and the son of man that you do care for him? Yet you have made him little less than God, and do crown him with glory and honor. . . . O Lord, our Lord, how majestic is your name in all the earth! Ps 8:3-9
Glory Be.

SCRIPTURE READING

No one has ascended into heaven but he who descended from heaven, the Son of man. And as Moses lifted up the serpent in the wilderness, so must the Son of man be lifted up, that whoever believes in him may have eternal life. Jn 3:13-15

Lord, may your Word be a lamp unto our feet,
And a light upon our path.

FAMILY INTERCESSIONS

Risen Savior, we thank you for your salvation and mercy upon our family, and pray for all our relatives who do not yet believe in you. *Lord, hear our prayer.*

Risen Savior, increase our love for those around us who are hungry, homeless, poor, wounded, blind, or disabled, and show us ways to express your love. *Lord, hear our prayer.*

Risen Savior, we pray for our other needs this day: (name them). *Lord, hear our prayer.*

THE LORD'S PRAYER & A HAIL MARY

MONDAY
WEEK TWO

OPENING PRAYER

In the name of the Father . . .

The Lord is my chosen portion and my cup; you hold my lot. The lines have fallen for me in pleasant places; yes, I have a goodly heritage. I bless the Lord who gives me counsel; in the night also my heart instructs me. I keep the Lord always before me; because he is at my right hand, I shall not be moved. **Ps 16:5-8**
Glory Be.

SCRIPTURE READING

And all who believed were together and had all things in common; and they sold their possessions and goods and distributed them to all, as any had need. And day by day, attending the temple together and breaking bread in their homes, they partook. of food with glad and generous hearts, praising God and having favor with all the people. And the Lord added to their number day by day those who were being saved. **Acts 2:44-47**

Lord, may your Word be a lamp unto our feet,
And a light upon our path.

FAMILY INTERCESSIONS

Risen Savior, you have indeed blessed our family abundantly. Grant that we may be good stewards of your many gifts and share with those in need. *Lord, hear our prayer.*

Risen Savior, grant that your people may grow in unity and love for one another, with a generous heart toward those who are less fortunate. Also, grant, risen Savior, that new believers be added to our number every day. *Lord, hear our prayer.*

Lord our God, hear our special needs: (name them).
Lord, hear our prayer.

THE LORD'S PRAYER & A HAIL MARY

TUESDAY
WEEK TWO

OPENING PRAYER

In the name of the Father . . .

Give the king your justice, O God, and your righteousness to the royal son! May he judge your people with righteousness, and your poor with justice! Let the mountains bear prosperity for the people, and the hills, in righteousness! May he defend the cause of the poor of the people, give deliverance to the needy, and crush the oppressor! **Ps 72:1-4**
Glory Be.

SCRIPTURE READING

"This is my commandment, that you love one another as I have loved you. Greater love has no man than this, that a man lay down his life for his friends. You are my friends if you do what I command you. No longer do I call you servants, for the servant does not know what his master is doing; but I have called you friends, for all that I have heard from my Father I have made known to you." **Jn 15:12-15**

Lord, may your Word be a lamp unto our feet,
And a light upon our path.

FAMILY INTERCESSIONS

Risen Savior, give our family hearts of obedience to your word so that we may truly be your friends. Teach us how to truly love one another. *Lord, hear our prayer.*

Risen Savior, you came into the world to bring deliverance. Teach us how to defend the cause of the poor, to serve those in need, and to bring justice to the oppressed. *Lord, hear our prayer.*

Risen Savior, hear our special requests: (name them).
Lord, hear our prayer.

THE LORD'S PRAYER & A HAIL MARY

WEDNESDAY
WEEK TWO

OPENING PRAYER

In the name of the Father . . .

I thank you that you have answered me and have become my salvation. The stone which the builders rejected has become the head of the corner. This is the Lord's doing; it is marvelous in our eyes. This is the day which the Lord has made; let us rejoice and be glad in it. **Ps 118:21-24**
Glory Be.

SCRIPTURE READING

Come to him, to that living stone, rejected by men but in God's sight chosen and precious; and like living stones be yourselves built into a spiritual house, to be a holy priesthood, to offer spiritual sacrifices acceptable to God through Jesus Christ. For it stands in Scripture: "Behold, I am laying in Zion a stone, a cornerstone chosen and precious, and he who believes in him will not be put to shame." **1 Pt 2:4-6**

Lord, may your Word be a lamp unto our feet,
And a light upon our path.

FAMILY INTERCESSIONS

Risen Savior, we offer our hearts to you as a spiritual sacrifice. Cleanse us and purify our family in the blood of your passion. *Lord, hear our prayer.*

Risen Savior, we pray with all the angels and saints that your church on earth be built into a strong spiritual house that offers true worship. *Lord, hear our prayer.*

Risen Savior, we bring our other needs to you this day: (name them). *Lord, hear our prayer.*

THE LORD'S PRAYER & A HAIL MARY

THURSDAY
WEEK TWO

OPENING PRAYER

In the name of the Father . . .

Blessed is the man who fears the Lord, who greatly delights in his commandments! His descendants will be mighty in the land; the generation of the upright will be blessed. Wealth and riches are in his house; and his righteousness endures for ever. Light rises in the darkness for the upright; the Lord is gracious, merciful, and righteous. **Ps 112:1-4**
Glory Be.

SCRIPTURE READING

"Truly, truly, I say to you, he who hears my word and believes him who sent me, has eternal life; he does not come into judgment, but has passed from death to life. Truly, truly, I say to you, the hour is coming, and now is, when the dead will hear the voice of the Son of God, and those who hear will live. For as the Father has life in himself, so he has granted the Son also to have life in himself, . . ."

Jn 5:24-27

Lord, may your Word be a lamp unto our feet,
And a light upon our path.

FAMILY INTERCESSIONS

Risen Savior, as a family we pray for ears to hear your voice and hearts that are quick to obey. We thank you for life in Jesus Christ and pray for a renewal of the grace of baptism. *Lord, hear our prayer.*

Risen Savior, we pray for all baptized believers, especially those who have fallen away and no longer seek you. Bring them back to your fold. *Lord, hear our prayer.*

Risen Savior, we pray for all of our needs this day, especially: (name them). *Lord, hear our prayer.*

THE LORD'S PRAYER & A HAIL MARY

FRIDAY
WEEK TWO

OPENING PRAYER

In the name of the Father . . .

The Lord swore to David a sure oath from which he will not turn back: "One of the sons of your body I will set on your throne. If your sons keep my covenant and my testimonies which I shall teach them, their sons also forever shall sit upon your throne."

Glory Be.   **Ps 132:11-12**

SCRIPTURE READING

He himself bore our sins in his body on the tree, that we might die to sin and live to righteousness. By his wounds you have been healed. For you were straying like sheep, but have now returned to the Shepherd and Guardian of your souls. **1 Pt 2:24-25**

Lord, may your Word be a lamp unto our feet,
And a light upon our path.

FAMILY INTERCESSIONS

Good Shepherd, give us strength to resist temptation and sin, and courage to suffer for our faith. Grant us greater obedience to you, the Shepherd and Guardian who willingly gave your life for us. *Lord, hear our prayer.*

Good Shepherd, we pray that your church would have greater hunger for righteousness, and that we might serve as witnesses to a dying world. *Lord, hear our prayer.*

Good Shepherd, we pray for our intentions of the day: (name them). *Lord, hear our prayer.*

THE LORD'S PRAYER & A HAIL MARY

SATURDAY
WEEK TWO

OPENING PRAYER

In the name of the Father . . .

O sing to the Lord a new song, for he has done marvelous things! His right hand and his holy arm have gotten him victory. The Lord has made known his victory, he has revealed his vindication in the sight of the nations. He has remembered his steadfast love and faithfulness to the house of Israel. All the ends of the earth have seen the victory of our God. **Ps 98:1-3**
Glory Be.

SCRIPTURE READING

For it was fitting that we should have such a high priest, holy, blameless, unstained, separated from sinners, exalted above the heavens. He has no need, like those high priests, to offer sacrifices daily, for his own sins and then for those of the people; he did this once for all when he offered up himself. **Heb 7:26-27**

Lord, may your Word be a lamp unto our feet,
And a light upon our path.

FAMILY INTERCESSIONS

Risen Savior, we pray that as a family we would offer up our lives to you as a daily sacrifice of praise, recognizing our priestly dignity as baptized believers. *Lord, hear our prayer.*

Risen Savior, equip the Holy Father, Pope (name), with all wisdom and love to shepherd the church as your vicar. Let all bishops and the priests they shepherd draw their strength from you, our high priest. *Lord, hear our prayer.*

Risen Savior, hear our special requests: (name them).
Lord, hear our prayer.

THE LORD'S PRAYER & A HAIL MARY

ASCENSION THURSDAY

OPENING PRAYER

In the name of the Father . . .

Clap your hands, all peoples! Shout to God with loud songs of joy! For the Lord, the Most High, is terrible, a great king over all the earth. . . . God has gone up with a shout, the Lord with the sound of a trumpet. Sing praises to God, sing praises! Sing praises to our King, sing praises! For God is the king of all the earth! Ps 47:1-7 *Glory Be.*

SCRIPTURE READING

As they were looking on, he was lifted up, and a cloud took him out of their sight. And while they were gazing into heaven as he went, behold, two men stood by them in white robes, and said, "Men of Galilee, why do you stand looking into heaven? This Jesus, who was taken up from you into heaven, will come in the same way as you saw him go into heaven." Acts 1:9-11

Lord, may your Word be a lamp unto our feet,
And a light upon our path.

FAMILY INTERCESSIONS

Glorified Lord, we worship and adore you as the king over all the earth. Grant us courage to be your faithful witnesses to all those we meet. Help us to keep our eyes fixed on heaven, to be looking for your coming again in glory. *Lord, hear our prayer.*

Glorified Lord, may all the faithful be more concerned with the things of above than with the temporary and short life we live here below. *Lord, hear our prayer.*

Glorified Lord, remember our special intentions: (name them). *Lord, hear our prayer.*

THE LORD'S PRAYER & A HAIL MARY

PENTECOST

OPENING PRAYER

In the name of the Father ...

O Lord, how manifold are your works! In wisdom you have made them all; the earth is full of your creatures.... When you send forth your Spirit, they are created; and you renew the face of the [earth]. May the glory of the Lord endure for ever, may the Lord rejoice in his works, who looks on the earth and it trembles, who touches the mountains and they smoke! Ps 104:24-32
Glory Be.

SCRIPTURE READING

When the day of Pentecost had come, they were all together in one place. And suddenly a sound came from heaven like the rush of a mighty wind, and it filled all the house where they were sitting. And there appeared to them tongues as of fire, distributed and resting on each one of them. And they were all filled with the Holy Spirit and began to speak in other tongues, as the Spirit gave them utterance. Acts 2:1-4

Lord, may your Word be a lamp unto our feet,
And a light upon our path.

FAMILY INTERCESSIONS

Father, send forth your Holy Spirit upon our family in a new and powerful way, that we may be empowered to live more fully in your joy and peace. *Lord, hear our prayer.*

Father, we pray for a fresh outpouring of your Holy Spirit upon all people, that hearts may be converted to you. *Lord, hear our prayer.*

Holy Spirit, help us to accomplish these special works today: (name them). *Lord, hear our prayer.*

THE LORD'S PRAYER & A HAIL MARY

Ordinary Time

EDITOR'S NOTE: A four-week cycle of daily entries has been provided for the thirty-three weeks of Ordinary Time. This time begins after the Christmas Season and is then interrupted by the Lenten and Easter Seasons. Ordinary Time resumes after Pentecost Sunday and runs until the first Sunday of Advent. There are many special feasts and solemnities that occur during Ordinary Time. Some of the feasts and solemnities that are of particular interest to families are provided in chapter six under Part Two.

SUNDAY
WEEK ONE

OPENING PRAYER

In the name of the Father . . .

When I look at your heavens, the work of your fingers, the moon and the stars which you have established; what is man that you are mindful of him, and the son of man that you care for him? Yet you have made him little less than God, and crown him with glory and honor. **Ps 8:3-5**
Glory Be.

SCRIPTURE READING

But you are a chosen race, a royal priesthood, a holy nation, God's own people, that you may declare the wonderful deeds of him who called you out of darkness into his marvelous light. Once you were no people but now you are God's people; once you had not received mercy but now you have received mercy. **1 Pt 2:9-10**

Lord, may your Word be a lamp unto our feet,
And a light upon our path.

FAMILY INTERCESSIONS

Heavenly Father, give our family eyes to see the many ways you have been merciful and loving to us. May we grow in our appreciation of your many blessings. *Lord, hear our prayer.*

Heavenly Father, we pray for your church, that we would be strengthened to walk in your light and to share with others about your love. *Lord, hear our prayer.*

Heavenly Father, we pray for our special intentions for this day: (name them). *Lord, hear our prayer.*

THE LORD'S PRAYER & A HAIL MARY

MONDAY
WEEK ONE

OPENING PRAYER

In the name of the Father . . .

To you I lift up my eyes, O you who are enthroned in the heavens! Behold, as the eyes of servants look to the hand of their master, as the eyes of a maid to the hand of her mistress, so our eyes look to the Lord our God, till he have mercy upon us. Have mercy upon us, O Lord, have mercy upon us, for we have had more than enough of contempt. **Ps 123:1-3**
Glory Be.

SCRIPTURE READING

Therefore, putting away falsehood, let every one speak the truth with his neighbor, for we are members one of another. Be angry but do not sin; do not let the sun go down on your anger, and give no opportunity to the devil. Let the thief no longer steal, but rather let him labor, doing honest work with his hands, so that he may be able to give to those in need. Let no evil talk come out of your mouths, but only such as is good for edifying, . . . **Eph 4:25-29**

Lord, may your Word be a lamp unto our feet,
And a light upon our path.

FAMILY INTERCESSIONS

Lord Jesus, guide our children who are in school that they may do well in their classes. Help those of us who work at home and in the marketplace to serve God and others humbly and honestly.
Lord, hear our prayer.

Lord Jesus, we pray for those who are unemployed. Grant them the means to support themselves and their families. *Lord, hear our prayer.*

Lord Jesus, we pray for our special needs as a family: (name them).
Lord, hear our prayer.

THE LORD'S PRAYER & A HAIL MARY

TUESDAY
WEEK ONE

OPENING PRAYER

In the name of the Father . . .

O God, you have rejected us, broken our defenses; you have been angry; oh, restore us, you have made the land to quake, you have rent it open; repair its breaches, for it totters. You have made your people suffer hard things; you have given us wine to drink that made us reel. **Ps 60:1-3**
Glory Be.

SCRIPTURE READING

Then the kings of the earth and the great men and the generals and the rich and the strong, and every one, slave and free, hid in the caves and among the rocks of the mountains, calling to the mountains and rocks, "Fall on us and hide us from the face of him who is seated on the throne, and from the wrath of the Lamb; for the great day of their wrath has come, and who can stand before it?"

Rv 6:15-17

Lord, may your Word be a lamp unto our feet,
And a light upon our path.

FAMILY INTERCESSIONS

Lord, strengthen our family's faith through difficulties and hard times. *Lord, hear our prayer.*

Lord, help all those who suffer the devastating effects of earthquakes or other disasters. Reveal yourself to all those who hold power and wealth in this world, that they may serve you and take refuge in you in the day of judgment. *Lord, hear our prayer.*

Lord, we pray for our personal needs this day: (name them).
Lord, hear our prayer.

THE LORD'S PRAYER & A HAIL MARY

WEDNESDAY
WEEK ONE

OPENING PRAYER

In the name of the Father . . .

Set a guard over my mouth, O Lord, keep watch over the door of my lips! Incline not my heart to any evil, to busy myself with wicked deeds in company with men who work iniquity; and let me not eat of their dainties! . . . But my eyes are toward you, O Lord God; in you I seek refuge; leave me not defenseless! **Ps 141:3-8** *Glory Be.*

SCRIPTURE READING

If we put bits into the mouths of horses that they may obey us, we guide their whole bodies. Look at the ships also; though they are so great and are driven by strong winds, they are guided by a very small rudder wherever the will of the pilot directs. So the tongue is a little member and boasts of great things. How great a forest is set ablaze by a small fire! And the tongue is a fire. The tongue is an unrighteous world among our members, staining the whole body, setting on fire the cycle of nature, and set on fire by hell. **Jas 3:3-6**

Lord, may your Word be a lamp unto our feet,
And a light upon our path.

FAMILY INTERCESSIONS

Lord Jesus, guard our tongues against gossip and other wrongful speech. Help us in our family to speak words that bring life to each other. *Lord, hear our prayer.*

Lord Jesus, we pray for those whose lives and reputations have been damaged by slander and gossip. May the cause of truth win out. *Lord, hear our prayer.*

Lord Jesus, we bring our specific needs before you this day: (name them). *Lord, hear our prayer.*

THE LORD'S PRAYER & A HAIL MARY

THURSDAY
WEEK ONE

OPENING PRAYER

In the name of the Father . . .

Come, bless the Lord, all you servants of the Lord, who stand by night in the house of the Lord! Lift up your hands to the holy place, and bless the Lord! May the Lord bless you from Zion, he who made heaven and earth! Ps 134
Glory Be.

SCRIPTURE READING

For here we have no lasting city, but we seek the city which is to come. Through him then let us continually offer up a sacrifice of praise to God, that is, the fruit of lips that acknowledge his name. Do not neglect to do good and to share what you have, for such sacrifices are pleasing to God. Obey your leaders and submit to them; for they are keeping watch over your souls, as men who will have to give account. Let them do this joyfully, and not sadly, for that would be of no advantage to you. Heb 13:14-17

Lord, may your Word be a lamp unto our feet,
And a light upon our path.

FAMILY INTERCESSIONS

Almighty God and Father, grant our family eyes of faith to see our eternal inheritance in Christ. We pray for generosity to share our earthly resources with others. *Lord, hear our prayer.*

Almighty God and Father, we pray for those who are homeless and hungry this day, that their needs would be met.
Lord, hear our prayer.

Almighty God and Father, we pray for our own needs as a family: (name them). *Lord, hear our prayer.*

THE LORD'S PRAYER & A HAIL MARY

FRIDAY
WEEK ONE

OPENING PRAYER

In the name of the Father . . .

O Lord, you will hear the desire of the meek; you will strengthen their heart, you will incline your ear to do justice to the fatherless and the oppressed, so that man who is of the earth may strike terror no more. Ps 10:17-18
Glory Be.

SCRIPTURE READING

We know that the whole creation has been groaning in travail together until now; and not only the creation, but we ourselves, who have the first fruits of the Spirit, groan inwardly as we wait for adoption as sons, the redemption of our bodies. For in this hope we were saved. Now hope that is seen is not hope. For who hopes for what he sees? But if we hope for what we do not see, we wait for it with patience. Rom 8:22-25

Lord, may your Word be a lamp unto our feet,
And a light upon our path.

FAMILY INTERCESSIONS

Loving Father, give us the grace and means as a family to help those in need in our neighborhood and parish community.
Lord, hear our prayer.

Loving Father, we pray for all those in prison, for those who suffer different forms of bondage, and for those who are confused. Protect those who are fatherless, widowed, or oppressed.
Lord, hear our prayer.

Loving Father, we pray for our special intentions for this day: (name them). *Lord, hear our prayer.*

THE LORD'S PRAYER & A HAIL MARY

SATURDAY
WEEK ONE

OPENING PRAYER

In the name of the Father . . .

May our sons in their youth be like plants full grown, our daughters like corner pillars cut for the structure of a palace; may our garners be full, providing all manner of store; may our sheep bring forth thousands and ten thousands in our fields; may our cattle be heavy with young, suffering no mischance or failure in bearing; may there be no cry of distress in our streets! Happy the people to whom such blessings fall! Happy the people whose God is the Lord! Ps 144:12-15
Glory Be.

SCRIPTURE READING

Finally, all of you, have unity of spirit, sympathy, love of the brethren, a tender heart, and a humble mind. Do not return evil for evil or reviling for reviling; but on the contrary bless, for to this you have been called, that you may obtain a blessing. . . . "For the eyes of the Lord are upon the righteous, and his ears are open to their prayer." 1 Pt 3:8-12a

Lord, may your Word be a lamp unto our feet,
And a light upon our path.

FAMILY INTERCESSIONS

Father, give us grace as a family to seek peace and pursue it with humble minds and tender hearts. *Lord, hear our prayer.*

Father, grant greater love and unity of spirit in the church, so that the world may believe that Jesus is the Son of God.
Lord, hear our prayer.

Father, hear our special needs for this day: (name them).
Lord, hear our prayer.

THE LORD'S PRAYER & A HAIL MARY

SUNDAY
WEEK TWO

OPENING PRAYER

In the name of the Father . . .

The Lord reigns; let the earth rejoice; let the many coastlands be glad! Clouds and thick darkness are round about him; righteousness and justice are the foundation of his throne. Fire goes before him, and burns up his adversaries round about. His lightnings lighten the world; the earth sees and trembles. **Ps 97:1-4**
Glory Be.

SCRIPTURE READING

"You are the light of the world. A city set on a hill cannot be hid. Nor do men light a lamp and put it under a bushel, but on a stand, and it gives light to all in the house. Let your light so shine before men, that they may see your good works and give glory to your Father who is in heaven." **Mt 5:14-16**

Lord, may your Word be a lamp unto our feet,
And a light upon our path.

FAMILY INTERCESSIONS

Heavenly Father, we pray for the strength and conviction to be a witness to the people in our neighborhood, at school, and at work, that they may know the forgiveness, love, and hope that Christ came to bring. May we give you glory in all that we do and say.
Lord, hear our prayer.

Heavenly Father, we pray for missionaries everywhere who seek to share the gospel. Grant them strength and perseverance.
Lord, hear our prayer.

Heavenly Father, grant our special intentions this day (name them). *Lord, hear our prayer.*

THE LORD'S PRAYER & A HAIL MARY

MONDAY
WEEK TWO

OPENING PRAYER

In the name of the Father . . .

Those who trust in the Lord are like Mount Zion, which cannot be moved, but abides for ever. As the mountains are round about Jerusalem, so the Lord is round about his people, from this time forth and for evermore. **Ps 125:1-2**
Glory Be.

SCRIPTURE READING

"You have heard that it was said, 'You shall not commit adultery.' But I say to you that every one who looks at a woman lustfully has already committed adultery with her in his heart. If your right eye causes you to sin, pluck it out and throw it away; it is better that you lose one of your members than that your whole body be thrown into hell. And if your right hand causes you to sin, cut it off and throw it away; it is better that you lose one of your members than that your whole body go into hell." **Mt 5:27-30**

Lord, may your Word be a lamp unto our feet,
And a light upon our path.

FAMILY INTERCESSIONS

Lord God, we pray for our family, that we would be pure of heart and mind. Grant us grace to repent and sin no more.
Lord, hear our prayer.

Lord God, we pray for the whole church, that we would be firmly established and rooted in you. We also pray for the Holy Father, Pope (name), and all the bishops, that they would be strong examples of faith and purity. *Lord, hear our prayer.*

Lord God, listen to our special needs today: (name them).
Lord, hear our prayer.

THE LORD'S PRAYER & A HAIL MARY

TUESDAY
WEEK TWO

OPENING PRAYER

In the name of the Father . . .

O Lord, my heart is not lifted up, my eyes are not raised too high; I do not occupy myself with things too great and too marvelous for me. But I have calmed and quieted my soul, like a child quieted at its mother's breast; like a child that is quieted is my soul. O Israel, hope in the Lord from this time forth and for evermore. **Ps 131**
Glory Be.

SCRIPTURE READING

At that time the disciples came to Jesus, saying, "Who is the greatest in the kingdom of heaven?" And calling to him a child, he put him in the midst of them, and said, "Truly, I say to you, unless you turn and become like children, you will never enter the kingdom of heaven. Whoever humbles himself like this child, he is the greatest in the kingdom of heaven." **Mt 18:1-4**

Lord, may your Word be a lamp unto our feet,
And a light upon our path.

FAMILY INTERCESSIONS

Heavenly Father, we ask a special blessing on our children, that you might protect them and let them experience your very personal love and care. *Lord, hear our prayer.*

Heavenly Father, we pray that all Christians would have true humility of heart and spirit as children of God. *Lord, hear our prayer.*

Heavenly Father, hear our special needs this day: (name them).
Lord, hear our prayer.

THE LORD'S PRAYER & A HAIL MARY

WEDNESDAY
WEEK TWO

OPENING PRAYER

In the name of the Father . . .

O Lord, you will hear the desire of the meek; you will strengthen their heart, you will incline your ear to do justice to the fatherless and the oppressed, so that man who is of the earth may strike terror no more. Ps 10:17-18
Glory Be.

SCRIPTURE READING

"You have heard that it was said to the men of old, 'You shall not kill; and whoever kills shall be liable to judgment.' But I say to you that every one who is angry with his brother shall be liable to judgment; whoever insults his brother shall be liable to the council, and whoever says, 'You fool!' shall be liable to the hell of fire. So if you are offering your gift at the altar, and there remember that your brother has something against you, leave your gift there before the altar and go; first be reconciled to your brother, and then come and offer your gift. Mt 5:21-24

Lord, may your Word be a lamp unto our feet,
And a light upon our path.

FAMILY INTERCESSIONS

Father, help us to forbear with one another in our family. May we always be ready to forgive and hold no grudges against each other.
Lord, hear our prayer.

Father, we pray for Christians around the world who are being oppressed, persecuted, or terrorized for their faith. Grant them strength and a speedy deliverance. *Lord, hear our prayer.*

Father, grant our particular needs this day: (name them).
Lord, hear our prayer.

THE LORD'S PRAYER & A HAIL MARY

THURSDAY
WEEK TWO

OPENING PRAYER

In the name of the Father . . .

There is a river whose streams make glad the city of God, the holy habitation of the Most High. God is in the midst of her, she shall not be moved; God will help her right early. The nations rage, the kingdoms totter; he utters his voice, the earth melts. The Lord of hosts is with us; the God of Jacob is our refuge. **Ps 46:4-7**
Glory Be.

SCRIPTURE READING

"Then will appear the sign of the Son of man in heaven, and then all the tribes of the earth will mourn, and they will see the Son of man coming on the clouds of heaven with power and great glory; and he will send out his angels with a loud trumpet call, and they will gather his elect from the four winds, from one end of heaven to the other." **Mt 24:30-31**

Lord, may your Word be a lamp unto our feet,
And a light upon our path.

FAMILY INTERCESSIONS

Lord Jesus, we acknowledge your majesty over our family and over all the kingdoms of this earth. We await the day when you will come in glory. *Lord, hear our prayer.*

Lord Jesus, strengthen your church to be faithful and persevere until your return. *Lord, hear our prayer.*

Lord Jesus, we bring you our other intentions: (name them).
Lord, hear our prayer.

THE LORD'S PRAYER & A HAIL MARY

FRIDAY
WEEK TWO

OPENING PRAYER

In the name of the Father . . .

How long, O Lord? Will you forget me for ever? How long will you hide your face from me? How long must I bear pain in my soul, and have sorrow in my heart all the day? How long shall my enemy be exalted over me? Consider and answer me, O Lord my God; . . .

Ps 13:1-3

Glory Be.

SCRIPTURE READING

Therefore take the whole armor of God, that you may be able to withstand in the evil day, and having done all, to stand. Stand therefore, having girded your loins with truth, and having put on the breastplate of righteousness, and having shod your feet with the equipment of the gospel of peace; besides all these, taking the shield of faith, with which you can quench all the flaming darts of the evil one. And take the helmet of salvation, and the sword of the Spirit, which is the word of God. Eph 6:13-17

Lord, may your Word be a lamp unto our feet,
And a light upon our path.

FAMILY INTERCESSIONS

Almighty God and Father, strengthen us as a family to do spiritual warfare and to stand firm against the forces of evil.
Lord, hear our prayer.

Almighty God and Father, strengthen all those who are in pain and sorrow, especially the mentally ill. Show them your salvation.
Lord, hear our prayer.

Almighty God and Father, we pray especially for: (name intentions).
Lord, hear our prayer.

THE LORD'S PRAYER & A HAIL MARY

SATURDAY
WEEK TWO

OPENING PRAYER

In the name of the Father . . .

It is good to give thanks to the Lord, to sing praises to your name, O Most High; to declare your steadfast love in the morning, and your faithfulness by night, to the music of the lute and the harp, to the melody of the lyre. For you, O Lord, have made me glad by your work; at the works of your hands I sing for joy. **Ps 92:1-4**
Glory Be.

SCRIPTURE READING

Pray at all times in the Spirit, with all prayer and supplication. To that end keep alert with all perseverance, making supplication for all the saints, and also for me, that utterance may be given me in opening my mouth boldly to proclaim the mystery of the gospel, for which I am an ambassador in chains; that I may declare it boldly, as I ought to speak. **Eph 6:18-20**

Lord, may your Word be a lamp unto our feet,
And a light upon our path.

FAMILY INTERCESSIONS

Heavenly Father, may our family ever sing your praises and rejoice in your constant goodness and love. May we join our voices with all the saints and angels, and with the faithful here below.
Lord, hear our prayer.

Heavenly Father, we pray for the church. Strengthen us all to be faithful and obedient disciples of Christ. *Lord, hear our prayer.*

Heavenly Father, grant our special petitions: (name them).
Lord, hear our prayer.

THE LORD'S PRAYER & A HAIL MARY

SUNDAY
WEEK THREE

OPENING PRAYER

In the name of the Father . . .

Who shall ascend the hill of the Lord? And who shall stand in his holy place? He who has clean hands and a pure heart, who does not lift up his soul to what is false, and does not swear deceitfully. He will receive a blessing from the Lord, and vindication from the God of his salvation. **Ps 24:3-5**
Glory Be.

SCRIPTURE READING

And an argument arose among them as to which of them was the greatest. But when Jesus perceived the thought of their hearts, he took a child and put him by his side, and said to them, "Whoever receives this child in my name receives me, and whoever receives me receives him who sent me; for he who is least among you all is the one who is great." **Lk 9:46-48**

Lord, may your Word be a lamp unto our feet,
And a light upon our path.

FAMILY INTERCESSIONS

Father, we pray for our family, that we may become the family that you want us to be. Help us to love you and one another from the heart. *Lord, hear our prayer.*

Father, we pray for the peace and safety of our country, and for peace throughout the world. *Lord, hear our prayer.*

Father, we pray for these special intentions of the day: (name them). *Lord, hear our prayer.*

THE LORD'S PRAYER & A HAIL MARY

MONDAY
WEEK THREE

OPENING PRAYER

In the name of the Father . . .

All the ends of the earth shall remember and turn to the Lord; and all the families of the nations shall worship before him. For dominion belongs to the Lord, and he rules over the nations.

Glory Be.   **Ps 22:27-28**

SCRIPTURE READING

Know therefore this day, and lay it to your heart, that the Lord is God in heaven above and on the earth beneath; there is no other. Therefore you shall keep his statutes and his commandments, which I command you this day, that it may go well with you, and with your children after you, and that you may prolong your days in the land which the Lord your God gives you forever. **Dt 4:39-40**

Lord, may your Word be a lamp unto our feet,
And a light upon our path.

FAMILY INTERCESSIONS

Lord Jesus, may our family members always obey and respect lawful authority, both religious and secular. *Lord, hear our prayer.*

Lord Jesus, bless the Holy Father, Pope (name), with your strength, wisdom, and guidance as he leads the church. Lord Jesus, bless also our (name President or Prime Minister) with good judgment in every decision he (or she) makes for our country.
Lord, hear our prayer.

Lord, we pray for our special intentions today: (name them).
Lord, hear our prayer.

THE LORD'S PRAYER & A HAIL MARY

TUESDAY
WEEK THREE

OPENING PRAYER

In the name of the Father . . .

Praise the Lord, O Jerusalem! Praise your God, O Zion! For he strengthens the bars of your gates; he blesses your sons within you. He makes peace in your borders; he fills you with the finest of the wheat. He sends forth his command to the earth; his word runs swiftly. Ps 147:12-15
Glory Be.

SCRIPTURE READING

Now the company of those who believed were of one heart and soul, and no one said that any of the things which he possessed was his own, but they had everything in common. And with great power the apostles gave their testimony to the resurrection of the Lord Jesus, and great grace was upon them all. Acts 4:32-33

Lord, may your Word be a lamp unto our feet,
And a light upon our path.

FAMILY INTERCESSIONS

Father, strengthen the parents of this family, give them (us) wisdom and guidance in directing the household.
Lord, hear our prayer.

Father, help Bishop (name local bishop), that he may receive from the Lord everything he needs to shepherd the people in this diocese. Also guide the members of our state and city governments, that they may serve the people wisely and justly.
Lord, hear our prayer.

Father, we bring before you our special intentions today: (name them). *Lord, hear our prayer.*

THE LORD'S PRAYER & A HAIL MARY

WEDNESDAY
WEEK THREE

OPENING PRAYER

In the name of the Father . . .

How precious is your steadfast love, O God! The children of men take refuge in the shadow of your wings. They feast on the abundance of your house, and you give them drink from the river of your delights. For with you is the fountain of life; in your light do we see light. **Ps 36:7-9**
Glory Be.

SCRIPTURE READING

"Truly, truly, I say to you, he who believes in me will also do the works that I do; and greater works than these will he do, because I go to the Father. Whatever you ask in my name, I will do it, that the Father may be glorified in the Son; if you ask anything in my name, I will do it." **Jn 14:12-14**

Lord, may your Word be a lamp unto our feet,
And a light upon our path.

FAMILY INTERCESSIONS

Father, grant all the children in our family good health and protect them from all harm. *Lord, hear our prayer.*

Father, bring about the unity of all Christians all over the world. Father, also protect all children and the unborn.
Lord, hear our prayer.

Father, we bring before you our special intentions for this day: (name them). *Lord, hear our prayer.*

THE LORD'S PRAYER & A HAIL MARY

THURSDAY
WEEK THREE

OPENING PRAYER

In the name of the Father . . .

Unless the Lord builds the house, those who build it labor in vain. Unless the Lord watches over the city, the watchman stays awake in vain. It is in vain that you rise up early and go late to rest, eating the bread of anxious toil; for he gives to his beloved sleep. Ps 127:1-2 *Glory Be.*

SCRIPTURE READING

The reward for humility and fear of the Lord is riches and honor and life. Thorns and snares are in the way of the perverse; he who guards himself will keep far from them. Train up a child in the way he should go, and when he is old he will not depart from it. Prv 22:4-6

Lord, may your Word be a lamp unto our feet,
And a light upon our path.

FAMILY INTERCESSIONS

Father, help us to train and form our children in your ways so that they may remain ever faithful to you. *Lord, hear our prayer.*

Lord, we pray that you would bless all the missionary work of the church around the world, that it may be successful in bringing people closer to you. *Lord, hear our prayer.*

Lord, we pray for all our family needs this day, especially: (name them). *Lord, hear our prayer.*

THE LORD'S PRAYER & A HAIL MARY

FRIDAY
WEEK THREE

OPENING PRAYER

In the name of the Father . . .

The Lord is your keeper; the Lord is your shade on your right hand. The sun shall not smite you by day, nor the moon by night. The Lord will keep you from all evil; he will keep your life. The Lord will keep your going out and your coming in from this time forth and for evermore. **Ps 121:5-8**
Glory Be.

SCRIPTURE READING

I write this to you who believe in the name of the Son of God, that you may know that you have eternal life. And this is the confidence which we have in him, that if we ask anything according to his will he hears us. And if we know that he hears us in whatever we ask, we know that we have obtained the requests made of him. **1 Jn 5:13-15**

Lord, may your Word be a lamp unto our feet,
And a light upon our path.

FAMILY INTERCESSIONS

Lord Jesus, protect our family from all evil influences in the world, and especially protect our children from embracing values that are not of you. *Lord, hear our prayer.*

Lord Jesus, give strength and perseverance to our brothers and sisters in Christ who are undergoing trials. Unloose your cleansing power on the moral problems in our country, especially those of abortion, pornography, and sexual immorality. Bring healing to all those who are hurting. *Lord, hear our prayer.*

Lord Jesus, hear our special needs today: (name them).
Lord, hear our prayer.

THE LORD'S PRAYER & A HAIL MARY

SATURDAY
WEEK THREE

OPENING PRAYER

In the name of the Father . . .

Teach us to number our days that we may get a heart of wisdom. . . . Let your work be manifest to your servants, and your glorious power to their children. Let the favor of the Lord our God be upon us, and may you establish the work of our hands. **Ps 90:12-17**
Glory Be.

SCRIPTURE READING

Be glad, O sons of Zion, and rejoice in the Lord, your God; for he has given the early rain for your vindication, he has poured down for you abundant rain, the early and the latter rain, as before. The threshing floors shall be full of grain, the vats shall overflow with wine and oil. **Jl 2:23-24**

Lord, may your Word be a lamp unto our feet,
And a light upon our path.

FAMILY INTERCESSIONS

Father, hear our family's financial and material needs (name some of them). *Lord, hear our prayer.*

Father, we pray for the conversion of all those who have hardened their hearts toward you, and we pray for our country, that we would be at peace with other nations around the world.
Lord, hear our prayer.

Father, help those who are most in need of financial help, especially: (name them). *Lord, hear our prayer.*

THE LORD'S PRAYER & A HAIL MARY

SUNDAY
WEEK FOUR

OPENING PRAYER

In the name of the Father . . .

O come, let us sing to the Lord; let us make a joyful noise to the rock of our salvation! Let us come into his presence with thanksgiving; let us make a joyful noise to him with songs of praise!

Glory Be.   **Ps 95:1-2**

SCRIPTURE READING

Let the word of Christ dwell in you richly, teach and admonish one another in all wisdom, and sing psalms and hymns and spiritual songs with thankfulness in your hearts to God. And whatever you do, in word or deed, do everything in the name of the Lord Jesus, giving thanks to God the Father through him.

Col 3:16-17

Lord, may your Word be a lamp unto our feet,
And a light upon our path.

FAMILY INTERCESSIONS

Heavenly Father, we pray for our family, that we would be ever thankful for the unity and life we share. *Lord, hear our prayer.*

Heavenly Father, we pray that the whole people of God may be filled with thanksgiving for your great mercies. May we be thankful for the very gift of life itself which enables us to know you. *Lord, hear our prayer.*

Heavenly Father, hear our special intentions for this day: (name them). *Lord, hear our prayer.*

THE LORD'S PRAYER & A HAIL MARY

MONDAY
WEEK FOUR

OPENING PRAYER

In the name of the Father . . .

Blessed be the Lord, who daily bears us up; God is our salvation. Our God is a God of salvation; and to God, the Lord, belongs escape from death. . . . Ascribe power to God, whose majesty is over Israel, and his power is in the skies. Terrible is God in his sanctuary, the God of Israel, he gives power and strength to his people. Blessed be God! **Ps 68:19-35**
Glory Be.

SCRIPTURE READING

Let love be genuine; hate what is evil, hold fast to what is good; love one another with brotherly affection; outdo one another in showing honor. Never flag in zeal, be aglow with the Spirit, serve the Lord. Rejoice in your hope, be patient in tribulation, be constant in prayer. **Rom 12:9-12**

Lord, may your Word be a lamp unto our feet,
And a light upon our path.

FAMILY INTERCESSIONS

Lord God, we pray that in our family we would outdo each other in loving and serving you. *Lord, hear our prayer.*

Lord God, we remember our Holy Father, Pope (name). Grant him unflagging zeal in loving and serving you. We pray also for the leader of our nation, (name), that your people may prosper under his (or her) rule. *Lord, hear our prayer.*

Lord God, we pray for these needs today: (name them).
Lord, hear our prayer.

THE LORD'S PRAYER & A HAIL MARY

TUESDAY
WEEK FOUR

OPENING PRAYER

In the name of the Father . . .

I will bless the Lord at all times; his praise shall continually be in my mouth. My soul makes its boast in the Lord; let the afflicted hear and be glad. O magnify the Lord with me, and let us exalt his name together! Ps 34:1-3
Glory Be.

SCRIPTURE READING

"Why do you call me 'Lord, Lord,' and not do what I tell you? Everyone who comes to me and hears my words and does them, I will show you what he is like: he is like a man building a house, who dug deep, and laid the foundation upon rock; and when a flood arose, the stream broke against that house, and could not shake it, because it had been well built." Lk 6:46-48

Lord, may your Word be a lamp unto our feet,
And a light upon our path.

FAMILY INTERCESSIONS

Father, we pray that we, the parents of this family, will have a deeper love for each other, good health, and strength to care for our children. *Lord, hear our prayer.*

Father, we pray for the bishops and the priests they shepherd, that they may be faithful and strong in preaching the gospel. We pray for a special blessing upon our bishop, (name of local bishop). *Lord, hear our prayer.*

Father, we pray for our special needs this day: (name them).
Lord, hear our prayer.

THE LORD'S PRAYER & A HAIL MARY

WEDNESDAY
WEEK FOUR

OPENING PRAYER

In the name of the Father . . .

The Lord is my shepherd, I shall not want; he makes me lie down in green pastures. He leads me beside still waters; he restores my soul. He leads me in paths of righteousness for his name's sake.

Ps 23:1-3

Glory Be.

SCRIPTURE READING

Do not be deceived; God is not mocked, for whatever a man sows, that he will also reap. For he who sows to his own flesh will from the flesh reap corruption; but he who sows to the Spirit will from the Spirit reap eternal life. And let us not grow weary in well-doing, for in due season we shall reap, if we do not lose heart.

Gal 6:7-9

Lord, may your Word be a lamp unto our feet,
And a light upon our path.

FAMILY INTERCESSIONS

Our loving Father, we pray for all the children in our family, that they would not grow weary of doing what is right. Help us, the parents, to be good examples of perseverance. *Lord, hear our prayer.*

Our loving Father, we pray for all the local pastors in the church, that they may serve you with zeal and power. We especially pray for the pastor of our parish, (name of parish). *Lord, hear our prayer.*

Our loving Father, we pray for these needs today: (name them). *Lord, hear our prayer.*

THE LORD'S PRAYER & A HAIL MARY

THURSDAY
WEEK FOUR

OPENING PRAYER

In the name of the Father . . .

O give thanks to the Lord, for he is good, for his steadfast love endures for ever. O give thanks to the God of gods, for his steadfast love endures forever. O give thanks to the Lord of lords, for his steadfast love endures for ever; to him who alone does great wonders, for his steadfast love endures for ever. Ps 136:1-4
Glory Be.

SCRIPTURE READING

Do not give yourself over to sorrow, and do not afflict yourself deliberately. Gladness of heart is the life of man, and the rejoicing of a man is length of days. Delight your soul and comfort your heart, and remove sorrow far from you, for sorrow has destroyed many, and there is no profit in it. Jealousy and anger shorten life, and anxiety brings on old age too soon. Sir 30:21-24

Lord, may your Word be a lamp unto our feet,
And a light upon our path.

FAMILY INTERCESSIONS

Lord Jesus, we pray that our life as a family would be characterized by abiding love for each other. *Lord, hear our prayer.*

Lord Jesus, we pray for all missionaries and Christian teachers, grant them perseverance in bringing the good news of your love and mercy to all. We also pray for the members of the lawmaking bodies in our country, national, state, and local, that they may pass laws that are good and just. *Lord, hear our prayer.*

Lord Jesus, we pray for all those who need our prayer today, especially: (name them). *Lord, hear our prayer.*

THE LORD'S PRAYER & A HAIL MARY

FRIDAY
WEEK FOUR

OPENING PRAYER

In the name of the Father . . .

Our soul waits for the Lord; he is our help and shield. Our heart is glad in him, because we trust in his holy name. May your steadfast love, O Lord, be upon us, even as we hope in you. Ps 33:20-22
Glory Be.

SCRIPTURE READING

May the God of steadfastness and encouragement grant you to live in such harmony with one another, in accord with Christ Jesus, that together you may with one voice glorify the God and Father of our Lord Jesus Christ. Welcome one another, therefore, as Christ has welcomed you, for the glory of God. Rom 15:5-7

Lord, may your Word be a lamp unto our feet,
And a light upon our path.

FAMILY INTERCESSIONS

Our God and Father, we pray for good health for all of us in this house. Protect us from illness and accidents. *Lord, hear our prayer.*

Our God and Father, we pray for the members of our parish community, (name of parish), that we may all be renewed in our faith. We further pray for all those who are poor, lonely, sick, forgotten, and oppressed, that they may be comforted and strengthened. *Lord, hear our prayer.*

Our God and Father, we bring to you all our other needs for this day: (name them). *Lord, hear our prayer.*

THE LORD'S PRAYER & A HAIL MARY

SATURDAY
WEEK FOUR

OPENING PRAYER

In the name of the Father . . .

It is good to give thanks to the Lord, to sing praises to your name, O Most High; to proclaim your kindness at dawn and your faithfulness throughout the night. For you make me glad, O Lord, by your deeds; at the works of your hands I rejoice. **Ps 92:1-4**
Glory Be.

SCRIPTURE READING

If my people who are called by my name humble themselves, and pray and seek my face, and turn from their wicked ways, then I will hear from heaven, and will forgive their sin and heal their land. Now my eyes will be open and my ears attentive to the prayer that is made in this place. **2 Chr 7:14-15**

Lord, may your Word be a lamp unto our feet,
And a light upon our path.

FAMILY INTERCESSIONS

Almighty God and Father, we remember our relatives, friends, and all those who have helped us this week. Draw them closer to you. *Lord, hear our prayer.*

Almighty God and Father, we pray for all the persecuted Christians all over the world. Comfort and strengthen them. We pray for peace in the world, especially in war-torn countries.
Lord, hear our prayer.

Almighty God and Father, we bring you our special needs for this day: (name them). *Lord, hear our prayer.*

THE LORD'S PRAYER & A HAIL MARY

Part Two

Special Feasts and Family Celebrations

Special Feasts and Solemnities

EDITOR'S NOTE: This chapter includes daily entries for a number of feasts and solemnities of particular interest to families throughout the church year.

THE FEAST OF THE BAPTISM OF THE LORD

*(On Sunday after the Epiphany; the feast is not held when
the Solemnity of the Epiphany is celebrated on January 7 or 8.)*

OPENING PRAYER

In the name of the Father . . .

Ascribe to the Lord, O heavenly beings, ascribe to the Lord glory
and strength. Ascribe to the Lord the glory of his name; worship the
Lord in holy array. The voice of the Lord is upon the waters; the
God of glory thunders, the Lord, upon many waters. The voice of
the Lord is powerful, the voice of the Lord is full of majesty. Ps 29:1-4
Glory Be.

SCRIPTURE READING

Then Jesus came from Galilee to the Jordan to John, to be baptized
by him. John would have prevented him, saying, "I need to be
baptized by you, and do you come to me?" But Jesus answered
him, "Let it be so now; for thus it is fitting for us to fulfill all
righteousness." Then he consented. And when Jesus was baptized,
he went up immediately from the water, and behold the heavens
were opened, and he saw the Spirit of God descending like a dove,
and alighting on him; and lo, a voice from heaven, saying, "This is
my beloved Son, with whom I am well pleased." Mt 3:13-17

Lord, may your Word be a lamp unto our feet,
And a light upon our path.

FAMILY INTERCESSIONS

Lord Jesus, we renew our baptismal vows to you. Help us to be
obedient and faithful to the Father's commands. *Lord, hear our prayer.*

Lord Jesus, we pray for all baptized believers, that they would
remain faithful to you. *Lord, hear our prayer.*

Lord Jesus, hear our special needs this day: (name them).
Lord, hear our prayer.

THE LORD'S PRAYER & A HAIL MARY

THE FEAST OF THE PRESENTATION
OF THE LORD
FEBRUARY 2

OPENING PRAYER

In the name of the Father . . .

Lift up your heads, O gates! and be lifted up, O ancient doors! that the King of glory may come in. Who is the King of glory? The Lord, strong and mighty, the Lord, mighty in battle! Lift up your heads, O gates! and be lifted up, O ancient doors! that the King of glory may come in. **Ps 24:7-9**
Glory Be.

SCRIPTURE READING

Now there was a man in Jerusalem, whose name was Simeon, and this man was righteous and devout, looking for the consolation of Israel, and the Holy Spirit was upon him. And it had been revealed to him by the Holy Spirit that he should not see death before he had seen the Lord's Christ. And inspired by the Spirit he came into the temple; and when the parents brought in the child Jesus, to do for him according to the custom of the law, he took him up in his arms and blessed God. **Lk 2:25-28**

Lord, may your Word be a lamp unto our feet,
And a light upon our path.

FAMILY INTERCESSIONS

Heavenly Father, thank you for the witness of Simeon and Anna, who saw Jesus as the Christ. Help our family to be righteous and devout, filled with your Holy Spirit. *Lord, hear our prayer.*

Heavenly Father, we pray that your church would be faithful and wait in joy for your return. *Lord, hear our prayer.*

Heavenly Father, we pray now for our special needs: (name them). *Lord, hear our prayer.*

THE LORD'S PRAYER & A HAIL MARY

THE SOLEMNITY OF ST. JOSEPH
MARCH 19

OPENING PRAYER

In the name of the Father . . .

Blessed is the man who fears the Lord, who greatly delights in his commandments! His descendants will be mighty in the land; the generation of the upright will be blessed. Wealth and riches are in his house; and his righteousness endures for ever. **Ps 112:1-3**
Glory Be.

SCRIPTURE READING

Now the birth of Jesus Christ took place in this way. When his mother Mary had been betrothed to Joseph, before they came together she was found to be with child of the Holy Spirit; and her husband Joseph, being a just man and unwilling to put her to shame, resolved to divorce her quietly. But as he considered this, behold, an angel of the Lord appeared to him in a dream, saying, "Joseph, son of David, do not fear to take Mary your wife, for that which is conceived in her is of the Holy Spirit; she will bear a son, and you shall call his name Jesus, for he will save his people from their sins." **Mt 1:18-21**

Lord, may your Word be a lamp unto our feet,
And a light upon our path.

FAMILY INTERCESSIONS

Heavenly Father, throught the intercession of St. Joseph, we pray that our dad, would be drawn closer to you. *Lord, hear our prayer.*

Heavenly Father, we pray for all fathers, that you would strengthen them in their call to lay down their lives for their wives and children. *Lord, hear our prayer.*

Heavenly Father, we bring before you our special requests: (name them). *Lord, hear our prayer.*

THE LORD'S PRAYER & A HAIL MARY

THE SOLEMNITY OF
THE ANNUNCIATION OF OUR LORD
MARCH 25

OPENING PRAYER

In the name of the Father . . .

Sacrifice and offering you do not desire; but you have given me an open ear. Burnt offering and sin offering you have not required. Then I said, "Lo, I come; in the roll of the book it is written of me; I delight to do your will, O my God; your law is within my heart."

Glory Be.   **Ps 40:6-8**

SCRIPTURE READING

And [the angel Gabriel] came to [Mary] and said, "Hail, O favored one, the Lord is with you!" But she was greatly troubled at the saying, and considered in her mind what sort of greeting this might be. And the angel said to her, "Do not be afraid, Mary, for you have found favor with God. And behold, you will conceive in your womb and bear a son, and you shall call his name Jesus.". . . And Mary said, "Behold, I am the handmaid of the Lord; let it be to me according to your word." And the angel departed from her. **Lk 1:28-38**

Lord, may your Word be a lamp unto our feet,
And a light upon our path.

FAMILY INTERCESSIONS

Almighty God, we thank you for the Savior, and for Mary's faith and humble willingness. Let all in this family believe your promises and be ready to say yes to you. *Lord, hear our prayer.*

Almighty God, may the church, ever inspired by Mary's obedience, say yes to you. *Lord, hear our prayer.*

Almighty God, with the help of Mary's intercession, we bring you our special needs: (name them). *Lord, hear our prayer.*

THE LORD'S PRAYER & A HAIL MARY

THE FEAST OF THE VISITATION
MAY 31

OPENING PRAYER

In the name of the Father . . .

Behold, God is my salvation; I will trust, and will not be afraid; for the Lord God is my strength and my song, and he has become my salvation. With joy you will draw water from the wells of salvation. And you will say in that day: "Give thanks to the Lord, call upon his name; make known his deeds among the nations, proclaim that his name is exalted." **Is 12:2-4**
Glory Be.

SCRIPTURE READING

In those days Mary arose and went with haste into the hill country, to a city of Judah, and she entered the house of Zechariah and greeted Elizabeth. And when Elizabeth heard the greeting of Mary, the babe leaped in her womb; and Elizabeth was filled with the Holy Spirit and she exclaimed with a loud cry, "Blessed are you among women, and blessed is the fruit of your womb!" **Lk 1:39-42**
Lord, may your Word be a lamp unto our feet,
And a light upon our path.

FAMILY INTERCESSIONS

Heavenly Father, thank you for Mary's example of humble service. Help our family to grow in expressing such love.
Lord, hear our prayer.

Heavenly Father, help the whole church to bring Christ to those we visit, to share the good news of Jesus by our love and concern for them. *Lord, hear our prayer.*

Heavenly Father, through the intercession of Mary, grant our petitions: (name them). *Lord, hear our prayer.*

THE LORD'S PRAYER & A HAIL MARY

THE SOLEMNITY OF THE ASSUMPTION
AUGUST 15

OPENING PRAYER

In the name of the Father . . .

The princess is decked in her chamber with gold-woven robes; in many-colored robes she is led to the king, with her virgin companions, her escort, in her train. With joy and gladness they are led along as they enter the palace of the king. Instead of your fathers shall be your sons; you will make them princes in all the earth. I will cause your name to be celebrated in all generations; therefore the peoples will praise you forever and ever. **Ps 45:13-17**
Glory Be.

SCRIPTURE READING

And Mary said, "My soul magnifies the Lord, and my spirit rejoices in God my Savior, for he had regarded the low estate of his handmaiden. For behold, henceforth all generations will call me blessed; for he who is mighty has done great things for me, and holy is his name." **Lk 1:46-49**

Lord, may your Word be a lamp unto our feet,
And a light upon our path.

FAMILY INTERCESSIONS

Lord Jesus, we praise you for the assumption of Mary into heaven, a sign of the hope of heaven for all of us. Grant all our family members grace to be faithful and obedient to you, that we too may one day come before you in glory. *Lord, hear our prayer.*

Lord Jesus, grant that all people would grow in their respect for the dignity and value of human life, recognizing that we are destined for glory. *Lord, hear our prayer.*

Lord Jesus, through the prayers of your mother, hear our special needs: (name them). *Lord, hear our prayer.*

THE LORD'S PRAYER & A HAIL MARY

THE FEAST OF THE BIRTH OF MARY
SEPTEMBER 8

OPENING PRAYER

In the name of the Father . . .

I have trusted in your steadfast love; my heart shall rejoice in your salvation. I will sing to the Lord, because he has dealt bountifully with me. **Ps 13:5-6**
Glory Be.

SCRIPTURE READING

Again the Lord spoke to Ahaz, "Ask a sign of the Lord your God; let it be deep as Sheol or high as heaven." But Ahaz said, "I will not ask, and I will not put the Lord to the test." And he said, "Hear then, O house of David! Is it too little for you to weary men, that you weary my God also? Therefore the Lord himself will give you a sign. Behold, a young woman shall conceive and bear a son, and shall call his name Immanuel." **Is 7:10-14**

Lord, may your Word be a lamp unto our feet,
And a light upon our path.

FAMILY INTERCESSIONS

Heavenly Father, we honor Mary this day, whom you prepared from the moment of conception to be the mother of your Son. Pour out your Holy Spirit upon us as a family, that we may serve you and give you glory through our lives. *Lord, hear our prayer.*

Heavenly Father, we pray for all the unborn, that you would protect them from harm. Blessed Virgin Mary, intercede for their safety. *Lord, hear our prayer.*

Heavenly Father, we bring you our special needs as a family: (name them). *Lord, hear our prayer.*

THE LORD'S PRAYER & A HAIL MARY

THE FEAST OF THE TRIUMPH OF THE CROSS
SEPTEMBER 14

OPENING PRAYER

In the name of the Father . . .

My heart is in anguish within me, the terrors of death have fallen upon me. Fear and trembling come upon me, and horror overwhelms me. . . . But I call upon God; and the Lord will save me. Evening and morning and at noon I utter my complaint and moan, and he will hear my voice. **Ps 55:4-17**
Glory Be.

SCRIPTURE READING

Christ Jesus, though he was in the form of God, did not count equality with God a thing to be grasped, but emptied himself, taking the form of a servant, being born in the likeness of men. And being found in human form he humbled himself and became obedient unto death, even death on a cross. Therefore God has highly exalted him and bestowed on him the name which is above every name, that at the name of Jesus every knee should bow, . . .

Phil 2:6-10

Lord, may your Word be a lamp unto our feet,
And a light upon our path.

FAMILY INTERCESSIONS

Lord Jesus, by the power of your cross may our family also share in your triumph. *Lord, hear our prayer.*

Lord Jesus, help all those suffering persecution around the world to be strengthened by your sacrifice on the cross.
Lord, hear our prayer.

Lord Jesus, hear our special needs today: (name them).
Lord, hear our prayer.

THE LORD'S PRAYER & A HAIL MARY

THE SOLEMNITY OF ALL SAINTS
NOVEMBER 1

OPENING PRAYER

In the name of the Father ...

Who shall ascend the hill of the Lord? And who shall stand in his holy place? He who has clean hands and a pure heart, who does not lift up his soul to what is false, and does not swear deceitfully. He will receive blessing from the Lord, and vindication from the God of his salvation. Ps 24:3-5
Glory Be.

SCRIPTURE READING

After this I looked, and behold, a great multitude which no man could number, from every nation, from all tribes and peoples and tongues, standing before the throne and before the Lamb, clothed in white robes, with palm branches in their hands, and crying out with a loud voice, "Salvation belongs to our God who sits upon the throne, and to the Lamb!" And all the angels stood round the throne and round the elders and the four living creatures, and they fell on their faces before the throne and worshiped God, ... Rv 7:9-11

Lord, may your Word be a lamp unto our feet,
And a light upon our path.

FAMILY INTERCESSIONS

Father, united in prayer with the saints in heaven, we pray for our family, that we may look beyond our material needs and seek heavenly things. *Lord, hear our prayer.*

Father, we pray that Christians undergoing trials may grow in perseverance, holiness, and faithfulness. *Lord, hear our prayer.*

Father, hear our specific intentions: (name them).
Lord, hear our prayer.

THE LORD'S PRAYER & A HAIL MARY

THE MEMORIAL OF ALL SOULS
NOVEMBER 2

OPENING PRAYER

In the name of the Father . . .

But the souls of the righteous are in the hand of God, and no torment will ever touch them. In the eyes of the foolish they seemed to have died, and their departure was thought to be an affliction, and their going from us to be their destruction; but they are at peace. For though in the sight of men they were punished, their hope is full of immortality. Having been disciplined a little, they will receive great good, because God tested them and found them worthy of himself. **Wis 3:1-5**
Glory Be.

SCRIPTURE READING

And I heard a voice from heaven saying, "Write this: Blessed are the dead who die in the Lord henceforth." "Blessed indeed," says the Spirit, "that they may rest from their labors, for their deeds follow them!" **Rv 14:13**

Lord, may your Word be a lamp unto our feet,
And a light upon our path.

FAMILY INTERCESSIONS

Lord, we especially remember our deceased relatives and friends. May they rest in peace. *Lord, hear our prayer.*

Lord, we pray for all those who have died in Christ, that they may enjoy the presence of God. We pray especially for all the souls in purgatory, that you would bring them into the joy of heaven. *Lord, hear our prayer.*

Lord, we bring before you specific requests: (name them). *Lord, hear our prayer.*

THE LORD'S PRAYER & A HAIL MARY

THE SOLEMNITY OF THE IMMACULATE CONCEPTION
DECEMBER 8

OPENING PRAYER

In the name of the Father . . .

O sing to the Lord a new song, for he has done marvelous things! His right hand and his holy arm have gotten him victory. The Lord has made known his victory, he has revealed his vindication in the sight of the nations. He has remembered his steadfast love and faithfulness to the house of Israel. **Ps 98:1-3**
Glory Be.

SCRIPTURE READING

We know that in everything God works for good with those who love him, who are called according to his purpose. For those whom he foreknew he also predestined to be conformed to the image of his Son, in order that he might be the firstborn among many brethren. And those whom he predestined he also called; and those whom he called he also justified; and those whom he justified he also glorified. **Rom 8:28-30**

Lord, may your Word be a lamp unto our feet,
And a light upon our path.

FAMILY INTERCESSIONS

Heavenly Father, we praise you for keeping Mary free of sin in preparation for the birth of Jesus. We pray that she will lead our family to her Son. *Lord, hear our prayer.*

Heavenly Father, through the intercession of Mary, we pray for pardon of all our sins and the sins of the world.
Lord, hear our prayer.

Heavenly Father, we pray for our special intentions for this day: (name them). *Lord, hear our prayer.*

THE LORD'S PRAYER & A HAIL MARY

Family Celebrations

EDITOR'S NOTE: This chapter includes daily entries for special family times and sacramental occasions.

BAPTISMS

OPENING PRAYER

In the name of the Father . . .

The Lord is my light and my salvation; whom shall I fear? The Lord is the stronghold of my life; of whom shall I be afraid? . . . One thing have I asked of the Lord, that will I seek after; that I may dwell in the house of the Lord all the days of my life, to behold the beauty of the Lord and to inquire in his temple. **Ps 27:1-4**
Glory Be.

SCRIPTURE READING

Do you not know that all of us who have been baptized into Christ Jesus were baptized into his death? We were buried therefore with him by baptism into death, so that as Christ was raised from the dead by the glory of the Father, we too might walk in newness of life. For if we have been united with him in a death like his, we shall certainly be united with him in a resurrection like his. **Rom 6:3-5**

Lord, may your Word be a lamp unto our feet,
And a light upon our path.

FAMILY INTERCESSIONS

Heavenly Father, we pray a special blessing upon (name of person being baptized), that you would continually show (him or her) the path of life. *Lord, hear our prayer.*

Heavenly Father, we praise you for the water which cleanses us of all impurity, through which we enter into the death and resurrection of Jesus Christ. *Lord, hear our prayer.*

Heavenly Father, we thank you for the gift of the Holy Spirit by which we become sons and daughters of God. *Lord, hear our prayer.*

THE LORD'S PRAYER & A HAIL MARY

BIRTHDAYS

OPENING PRAYER

In the name of the Father . . .

O Lord, you have searched me and known me! . . . For you did form my inward parts, you did knit me together in my mother's womb. I praise you, for you are fearful and wonderful. Wonderful are your works! Ps 139:1-14
Glory Be.

SCRIPTURE READING

The eyes of the Lord are upon those who love him, a mighty protection and strong support, a shelter from the hot wind and a shade from noonday sun, a guard against stumbling and a defense against falling. He lifts up the soul and gives light to the eyes; he grants healing, life, and blessing. Sir 34:16-17

Lord, may your Word be a lamp unto our feet,
And a light upon our path.

FAMILY INTERCESSIONS

Heavenly Father, we ask your special blessing on (name of birthday celebrant) this day, according to your abundant promises. We also pray that you would grant (name) long life, filled with the knowledge of your saving love. *Lord, hear our prayer.*

Heavenly Father, we thank you and praise you for the precious gift of life, and especially eternal life in Jesus Christ. May all Christians cherish this great gift. *Lord, hear our prayer.*

Heavenly Father, we ask for a joyous birthday celebration, that through it you would increase our love for one another.
Lord, hear our prayer.

THE LORD'S PRAYER & A HAIL MARY

NAME DAYS

(Your name day is the feast day of the saint you were named after.)

OPENING PRAYER

In the name of the Father . . .

When I look at your heavens, the work of your fingers, the moon and stars which you have established; what is man that you are mindful of him, and the son of man that you do care for him? Yet you have made him little less than God, and do crown him with glory and honor. **Ps 8:3-5**
Glory Be.

SCRIPTURE READING

But now thus says the Lord, he who created you, O Jacob, he who formed you, O Israel: "Fear not, for I have redeemed you; I have called you by name, you are mine. When you pass through the waters I will be with you; and through the rivers, they shall not overwhelm you; when you walk through fire you shall not be burned, and the flame shall not consume you. For I am the Lord your God, the Holy One of Israel, your Savior." **Is 43:1-3a**

Lord, may your Word be a lamp unto our feet,
And a light upon our path.

FAMILY INTERCESSIONS

Father, give (name of today's celebrant) a deeper understanding of the meaning and character of the name he or she bears.
Lord, hear our prayer.

Most gracious and loving Father, we thank you for creating us and calling us by name even before we were born.
Lord, hear our prayer.

Father, we pray for the grace to live up to the name and calling that you have given to us. *Lord, hear our prayer.*

THE LORD'S PRAYER & A HAIL MARY

FIRST COMMUNION

OPENING PRAYER

In the name of the Father . . .

The Lord is faithful in all his words, and gracious in all his deeds. The Lord upholds all who are falling, and raises up all who are bowed down. The eyes of all look to you, and you give them their food in due season. You open your hand, you satisfy the desire of every living thing. **Ps 145:13a-16**
Glory Be.

SCRIPTURE READING

For I received from the Lord what I also delivered to you, that the Lord Jesus on the night when he was betrayed took bread, and when he had given thanks, he broke it, and said, "This is my body which is for you. Do this in remembrance of me." In the same way also the cup, after supper, saying, "This cup is the new covenant in my blood. Do this, as often as you drink it, in remembrance of me." For as often as you eat this bread and drink the cup, you proclaim the Lord's death until he comes. **1 Cor 11:23-26**

Lord, may your Word be a lamp unto our feet,
And a light upon our path.

FAMILY INTERCESSIONS

Heavenly Father, we thank you for (name of family's first communicant), especially for his or her faith in Jesus. We ask you to pour out your grace upon him or her this day. *Lord, hear our prayer.*

Heavenly Father, we thank you and praise you for the Eucharist, for the gift of the Body and Blood of your Son, Jesus Christ, who died for us. *Lord, hear our prayer.*

Heavenly Father, we ask your special blessing on all of today's first communicants, that you would help them to grow in faith and love. *Lord, hear our prayer.*

THE LORD'S PRAYER & A HAIL MARY

CONFIRMATION

OPENING PRAYER

In the name of the Father . . .

The Lord is my shepherd, I shall not want; he makes me lie down in green pastures. He leads me beside still waters; he restores my soul. He leads me in paths of righteousness for his name's sake. Even though I walk through the valley of the shadow of death, I fear no evil; for you are with me; your rod and your staff, they comfort me.

Ps 23:1-4

Glory Be.

SCRIPTURE READING

Now there are varieties of gifts, but the same Spirit; and there are varieties of service, but the same Lord; and there are varieties of working, but it is the same God who inspires them all in every one. To each is given the manifestation of the Spirit for the common good. . . . All these are inspired by one and the same Spirit, who apportions to each one individually as he wills. **1 Cor 12:4-11**

Lord, may your Word be a lamp unto our feet,
And a light upon our path.

FAMILY INTERCESSIONS

Heavenly Father, we pray a special blessing on those newly confirmed this day, especially (name of family member).
Lord, hear our prayer.

Heavenly Father, we pray for a fresh anointing of the Holy Spirit upon all those who have been confirmed. *Lord, hear our prayer.*

Heavenly Father, we pray for a greater openness to the work of your Spirit in the church, that your power and gifts may bring us into greater unity and love. *Lord, hear our prayer.*

THE LORD'S PRAYER & A HAIL MARY

GRADUATION

OPENING PRAYER

In the name of the Father . . .

I give you thanks, O Lord, with my whole heart; before the gods I sing your praise; I bow down toward your holy temple and give thanks to your name for your steadfast love and your faithfulness; for you have exalted above everything your name and your word. On the day I called, you did answer me, my strength of soul you did increase. . . . The Lord will fulfill his purpose for me; your steadfast love, O Lord, endures for ever. **Ps 138**
Glory Be.

SCRIPTURE READING

Trust in the Lord with all your heart, and do not rely on your own insight. In all your ways acknowledge him, and he will make straight your paths. Be not wise in your own eyes; fear the Lord, and turn away from evil. It will be healing to your flesh and refreshment to your bones. Honor the Lord with your substance and with the first fruits of all your produce; then your barns will be filled with plenty, and your vats will be bursting with wine.

Prv 3:5-10

Lord, may your Word be a lamp unto our feet,
And a light upon our path.

FAMILY INTERCESSIONS

Lord our God, we thank you for your faithfulness to (name of graduate), and for his or her perseverance and good work.
Lord, hear our prayer.

Lord our God, we pray for (name of graduate), that you would lead and guide him or her in the months and years to come.
Lord, hear our prayer.

Lord our God, we pray especially for wisdom from above and greater trust in you. *Lord, hear our prayer.*

THE LORD'S PRAYER & A HAIL MARY

WEDDING ANNIVERSARY

OPENING PRAYER

In the name of the Father . . .

Blessed is every one who fears the Lord, who walks in his ways! You shall eat the fruit of the labor of your hands; you shall be happy, and it shall be well with you. Your wife will be like a fruitful vine within your house; your children will be like olive shoots around your table. Lo, thus shall the man be blessed who fears the Lord. **Ps 128:1-4**
Glory Be.

SCRIPTURE READING

And Pharisees came up to him and tested him by asking, "Is it lawful to divorce one's wife for any cause?" He answered, "Have you not read that he who made them from the beginning made them male and female, and said, 'For this reason a man shall leave his father and mother and be joined to his wife, and the two shall become one flesh'? So they are no longer two but one flesh. What therefore God has joined together, let not man put asunder."

Mt 19:3-6

Lord, may your Word be a lamp unto our feet,
And a light upon our path.

FAMILY INTERCESSIONS

Lord Jesus Christ, we pray for greater joy and fruitfulness in our marriage. *Lord, hear our prayer.*

Lord Jesus Christ, we pray for all Christian marriages, for grace to remain faithful until death, and for deeper unity and love between husbands and wives. *Lord, hear our prayer.*

Lord Jesus Christ, we pray for those couples who are having difficulties in their married life. *Lord, hear our prayer.*

THE LORD'S PRAYER & A HAIL MARY

THE ANNIVERSARY OF THE DEATH OF A LOVED ONE

OPENING PRAYER

In the name of the Father . . .

For God alone my soul waits in silence; from him comes my salvation. He only is my rock and my salvation, my fortress. I shall not be greatly moved. **Ps 62:1-2**
Glory Be.

SCRIPTURE READING

For God so loved the world that he gave his only Son, that whoever believes in him should not perish but have eternal life. For God sent the Son into the world, not to condemn the world, but that the world might be saved through him. **Jn 3:16-17**

Lord, may your Word be a lamp unto our feet,
And a light upon our path.

FAMILY INTERCESSIONS

Risen Savior, we thank you for (name of deceased) and the witness of (his/her) life in you. May (he/she) receive your gracious forgiveness and enjoy eternal life with you, and all the saints and angels in heaven. *Lord, hear our prayer.*

Risen Savior, we pray for all the faithfully departed, especially those whom we now remember (name other deceased family members and friends). Grant them rest and full communion with you in heaven. *Lord, hear our prayer.*

Risen Savior, we pray that you would console all those who are mourning the loss of a loved one, especially (name those closest to the deceased loved one whose anniversary it is). May their mourning be turned into joy as they contemplate the unsurpassable happiness of heaven. *Lord, hear our prayer.*

THE LORD'S PRAYER & A HAIL MARY

MOTHER'S DAY

OPENING PRAYER

In the name of the Father . . .

Come, bless the Lord, all you servants of the Lord, who stand by night in the house of the Lord! Lift up your hands to the holy place, and bless the Lord! May the Lord bless you from Zion, he who made heaven and earth! **Ps 134**
Glory Be.

SCRIPTURE READING

A good wife who can find? She is far more precious than jewels. The heart of her husband trusts in her, and he will have no lack of gain. She does him good, and not harm, all the days of her life. . . . Strength and dignity are her clothing, and she laughs at the time to come. She opens her mouth with wisdom, and the teaching of kindness is on her tongue. She looks well to the ways of her household, and does not eat the bread of idleness. Her children rise up and call her blessed; her husband also, and he praises her: "Many women have done excellently, but you surpass them all."
Prv 31:10-29

Lord, may your Word be a lamp unto our feet,
And a light upon our path.

FAMILY INTERCESSIONS

Heavenly Father, we thank you for our mother and ask your special blessing upon her this day. Grant her joy, long life, wisdom, and good health. *Lord, hear our prayer.*

Heavenly Father, we pray for all Christian mothers, that you would help them to grow in likeness to Mary, especially in her love, faith, and caring spirit. *Lord, hear our prayer.*

Heavenly Father, help us to honor our mother this day and every day. *Lord, hear our prayer.*

THE LORD'S PRAYER & A HAIL MARY

FATHER'S DAY

OPENING PRAYER

In the name of the Father . . .

Blessed is the man who walks not in the counsel of the wicked, nor stands in the way of sinners, nor sits in the seat of scoffers; but his delight is in the law of the Lord, and on his law he meditates day and night. He is like a tree planted by streams of water, that yields its fruit in its season, and its leaf does not wither. In all that he does, he prospers. Ps 1:1-3
Glory Be.

SCRIPTURE READING

Listen to me your father, O children; and act accordingly, that you may be kept in safety. For the Lord honored the father above the children, and he confirmed the right of the mother over her sons. Whoever honors his father atones for sins, and whoever glorifies his mother is like one who lays up treasure. Whoever honors his father will be gladdened by his own children, and when he prays he will be heard. Whoever [reveres] his father will have long life, and whoever obeys the Lord will refresh his mother; he will serve his parents as his masters. Sir 3:1-7

Lord, may your Word be a lamp unto our feet,
And a light upon our path.

FAMILY INTERCESSIONS

Heavenly Father, we thank you for the gift of our father and pray that you would grant him wisdom, health, success, long life, and joy in his family. *Lord, hear our prayer.*

Heavenly Father, we pray for all Christian fathers, that you would draw them ever closer to Jesus. *Lord, hear our prayer.*

Heavenly Father, help us to honor our father this day and every day. *Lord, hear our prayer.*

THE LORD'S PRAYER & A HAIL MARY

THANKSGIVING DAY

OPENING PRAYER

In the name of the Father . . .

When the Lord restored the fortunes of Zion, we were like those who dream. Then our mouth was filled with laughter, and our tongue with shouts of joy; then they said among the nations, "The Lord has done great things for them." The Lord has done great things for us; we are glad. **Ps 126:1-3**
Glory Be.

SCRIPTURE READING

Rejoice in the Lord always; again I will say, Rejoice. Let all men know your forbearance. The Lord is at hand. Have no anxiety about anything, but in everything by prayer and supplication with thanksgiving let your requests be made known to God. And the peace of God, which passes all understanding, will keep your hearts and your minds in Christ Jesus. **Phil 4:4-7**

Lord, may your Word be a lamp unto our feet,
And a light upon our path.

FAMILY INTERCESSIONS

Heavenly Father, we are especially thankful this day for all of your many blessings to our family over the past year. You have been so faithful to us. *Lord, hear our prayer.*

Heavenly Father, we pray for grace to rejoice always and to make known our needs to you with thanksgiving, knowing that you hear our prayers. *Lord, hear our prayer.*

Heavenly Father, we pray for greater joy, peace, and harmony in our home, that we may glorify you. *Lord, hear our prayer.*

THE LORD'S PRAYER & A HAIL MARY

Appendices

Appendices

Prayers for Your Family and Relatives

PRAYER FOR THE FAMILY

Heavenly Father, we thank you for the gift of our family. Bless us this day as we seek to please you. May we grow in love for each other and build one another up in Christ. Grant us your loving guidance and order for our family life. May our home reflect the peace of Christ as we strive to be of one heart and mind. We entrust all of our needs to you, for you are faithful. We ask this through Christ our Lord. *Amen.*

PRAYER FOR FATHER

Our loving and gracious God, we thank you for Dad, the father of our family. We thank you for the way he reflects your goodness, faithfulness, fatherly love, and protection in caring for us. (*Add particular blessings that come to the family through Dad*). We ask you, almighty and loving Father, to give him wisdom, power, and strength as he leads us. Make him more and more a man after your own heart, confident in your loving plan for us as a family. We ask this through Christ our Lord. *Amen.*

PRAYER FOR MOTHER

We ask your intercession before God, O Blessed Virgin Mary, for Mom, the mother of our family. We are grateful for the many ways she generously gives herself to us, bringing life, peace, and joy into our midst. (*Add particular blessings that come to the family through Mom.*) May her loving labors be rewarded. We entreat you to pray, holy Mother of God, that all of her daily sacrifices for us will bear much fruit for your Son, Jesus. Grant that she may know more deeply your Son's tender love for her. And grant that she may entrust each of us into your loving care. We ask this through Christ our Lord. *Amen.*

PRAYER FOR SON

Lord Jesus Christ, only Son of the Father, we thank you for the gift of our son (name). What a blessing he is to all of us. (*Insert particular ways in which he is a blessing to the family.*) We ask that he would grow into a strong and mature young man, filled with love for you and ready to serve your church. Lord Jesus, Son of the living God, we ask that you would bring him into the fullness of life in your Holy Spirit, as he seeks you in prayer and receives you in word and sacrament. We ask this through Christ our Lord. *Amen.*

PRAYER FOR DAUGHTER

We entrust our daughter into your loving care, O Blessed Virgin Mary. How blessed we are to have (name) as our daughter! We delight in the great gift that she is to the entire family. (*Mention some of the ways she has blessed your family.*) O Mother of God, you who received Christ into your womb when you were tender in years, pray that she might know how much you and your Son, Jesus, dearly love her. May she mature into a strong young woman, whose heart is filled with love for God and his people. May she be brought into the fullness of life in the Holy Spirit, as she seeks your Son in prayer and receives him in word and sacrament. We ask this through Christ our Lord. *Amen.*

PRAYER FOR GRANDFATHER

Heavenly Father, we thank you for Grandpa (name). You have always been his sure help and provided for all his needs. We pray, Lord, for abundant grace for him. May he draw even closer to you as he advances in age. Fill him with your joy and peace, and grant him a thankful heart for everything that you have done in his life. We ask this through Christ our Lord. *Amen.*

PRAYER FOR GRANDMOTHER

We ask your intercession, O Blessed Virgin Mary, for Grandma (name). Her steadfast obedience and faithfulness over the years have been such an example for all of us! As she advances in age, we pray that she may continue to have faith that God will meet her every need. We entreat you to pray, holy Mother of God, that she would know God's love for her in a special way through your Son, Jesus. Give her continued joy and a sure hope in the completion of your plan for her life. We ask this through Christ our Lord. *Amen.*

PRAYER FOR UNCLE

Almighty Father, remember Uncle (name). We thank you that he is a part of our family. Pour out your grace upon him and continue to show him your plan for his life. Give him all the gifts that he needs to pursue it and grant him success in the work of his hands. Let him live to a ripe old age, full of joy. We ask this through Christ our Lord. *Amen.*

PRAYER FOR AUNT

We ask your intercession, O Blessed Virgin Mary, for Aunt (name). We are grateful for the gift that she is to our family. Beseech your Son on her behalf, that she may be more secure in Christ's love for her. O Mother of God, grant her greater peace and joy in her work. May she seek that God's will be accomplished in her life. Watch over her in all her undertakings, and reward the work of her hands! We ask this through Christ our Lord. *Amen.*

PRAYER FOR COUSIN

Father in heaven, we bring our cousin (name) before you. We thank you for the joy he (or she) has brought us. Father, we pray for an outpouring of your blessing and mercy upon (name). Let him (or her) experience your grace to meet any need. We ask this through Christ our Lord. *Amen.*

Traditional Catholic Prayers

THE ANGELUS

The angel of the Lord declared unto Mary:
And she conceived of the Holy Spirit.
Hail Mary . . .

Behold the handmaid of the Lord:
Be it done unto me according to your word.
Hail Mary . . .

And the Word was made flesh:
And dwelt among us.
Hail Mary . . .

Pray for us, O holy Mother of God,
That we may be worthy of the promises of Christ.

Let us pray. Pour forth, we beseech you, O Lord, your grace into our hearts, that we, to whom the incarnation of Christ, your Son, was made known by the message of an angel, may be brought by his passion and cross to the glory of his resurrection through the same Christ our Lord. *Amen.*

May the divine assistance remain always with us and may the souls of the faithful departed, through the mercy of God, rest in peace. *Amen.*

THE APOSTLE'S CREED

I believe in God, the Father almighty, creator of heaven and earth, and in Jesus Christ, his only Son, our Lord, who was conceived by the Holy Spirit, born of the Virgin Mary, suffered under Pontius Pilate, was crucified, died, and was buried. He descended into hell. The third day he rose again from the dead. He ascended into heaven, and sits at the right hand of God the Father almighty. From thence he shall come to judge the living and the dead. I believe in the Holy Spirit, the holy Catholic Church, the Communion of Saints, the forgiveness of sins, the resurrection of the body, and life everlasting. *Amen.*

CANTICLE OF ZECHARIAH (Benedictus)

Blessed be the Lord God of Israel,
for he has visited and redeemed his people,
and has raised up a horn of salvation
for us in the house of his servant David,
as he spoke by the mouth of his holy prophets from of old,
that we should be saved from our enemies,
and from the hand of all who hate us;
to perform the mercy promised to our fathers,
and to remember his holy covenant,
the oath which he swore to our father Abraham,
to grant us that we, being delivered from our enemies,
might serve him without fear,
in holiness and righteousness before him all the days of our life.

And you, child, will be called the prophet of the Most High;
for you will go before the Lord to prepare his ways,
to give knowledge of salvation to his people
in the forgiveness of their sins,
through the tender mercy of our God,
when the day shall dawn upon us from on high to give light to
those who sit in darkness and in the shadow of death,
to guide our feet into the way of peace. Lk 1:68-79

COME HOLY SPIRIT

Come, Holy Spirit, fill the hearts of your faithful, and enkindle in them the fire of your love. Send forth your Spirit and they shall be created, and you shall renew the face of the earth. Let us pray. O God, who has taught the hearts of the faithful by the light of the Holy Spirit, grant that by the gift of the same Spirit we may be always truly wise and ever rejoice in his consolation.

DIVINE PRAISES (Te Deum)

You are God, we praise you.
  You are the Lord: we acclaim you.
You are the eternal Father:
  all creation worships you.

To all angels, all the powers of heaven,
cherubim and seraphim, sing in endless praise:
  Holy, holy, holy Lord, God of power and might,
  heaven and earth are full of your glory.

The glorious company of apostles praise you.
  The noble fellowship of prophets praise you.
  The white-robed army of martyrs praise you.

Throughout the world the holy church acclaims you:
  Father, of majesty unbounded,
  your true and only Son, worthy of all worship,
  and the Holy Spirit, advocate and guide.

You, Christ, are the King of glory,
  eternal Son of the Father.
When you became man to set us free,
  you did not disdain the Virgin's womb.

You overcame the sting of death
  and opened the kingdom of heaven to all believers.
You are seated at God's right hand in glory.
  We believe that you will come and be our judge.

Come, then, Lord, sustain your people,
   bought with the price of your own blood,
and bring us with your saints
   to everlasting glory.

Glory be to the Father
   and to the Son
   and to the Holy Spirit.
As it was in the beginning
   is now and ever shall be,
   world without end. Amen.

The Gloria

Glory to God in the highest,
   and peace to his people on earth.
Lord God, heavenly King, almighty God and Father,
   we worship you, we give you thanks,
   we praise you for your glory.
Lord Jesus Christ, only Son of the Father,
Lord God, Lamb of God,
   you take away the sin of the world:
   have mercy on us;
   you are seated at the right hand of the Father,
   receive our prayer.
For you alone are the Holy One,
   you alone are the Lord,
   you alone are the Most High, Jesus Christ,
   with the Holy Spirit,
   in the glory of God the Father. *Amen.*

Grace before Meals

Bless us, O Lord, and these your gifts which we are about to receive
from your bounty, through Christ our Lord. *Amen.*

Grace after Meals

We give you thanks for all your benefits (gifts), almighty God, who
lives and reigns, forever and ever. *Amen.*

THE JESUS PRAYER

Lord Jesus Christ,
Son of the living God,
Have mercy on me, a sinner.

HAIL, HOLY QUEEN

Hail, holy Queen, mother of Mercy.
Hail, our life, our sweetness, and our hope.
To you do we cry, poor banished children of Eve;
to you do we send up our sighs, mourning and weeping,
    in this vale of tears.
Turn then, most gracious advocate, your eyes of mercy
    toward us;
and after this our exile, show unto us the blessed
fruit of your womb, Jesus. O clement, O loving,
O sweet Virgin Mary.

Pray for us, O holy Mother of God,
that we may be made worthy of the promises of Christ.

Let us pray:
Almighty, everlasting God, who through the working of the Holy
Spirit, prepared the body and soul of the glorious Virgin Mary to be
a worthy dwelling for your Son: grant that we who remember her
with joy may be delivered by her prayers from the evils that beset
us in this world and from everlasting death in the next. Through
the same Christ our Lord. *Amen.*

THE HAIL MARY

Hail Mary, full of grace,
the Lord is with you.
Blessed are you among women,
and blessed is the fruit of your womb, Jesus.
Holy Mary, Mother of God,
pray for us sinners, now,
and at the hour of our death.
Amen.

MAGNIFICAT

My soul glorifies the Lord,
and my spirit rejoices in God my Savior.
He has regarded the low estate of his handmaiden;
henceforth all generations will call me blessed.
For he who is mighty has done great things for me,
and holy is his name.
His mercy is from age to age,
on those who fear him.
He puts forth his arm in strength
and scatters the mighty from their thrones
and raises the lowly.
He fills the hungry with good things,
and the rich he sends away empty.
He protects Israel his servant,
remembering his mercy,
the mercy promised to our fathers,
to Abraham and his sons for ever. Lk 1:46-55

THE MEMORARE

Remember, O most loving Virgin Mary, that never was it known
that anyone who fled to your protection, implored your help, or
sought your intercession was left unaided. Inspired by this
confidence, we fly unto you, O virgin of virgins, our Mother. To you
we come, before you we stand, sinful and sorrowful. O Mother of
the Word incarnate, despise not our petitions, but in your mercy
hear and answer me.

THE FIFTEEN MYSTERIES OF THE ROSARY

(Each mystery is recited by praying one Our Father, ten Hail
Marys, and one Glory Be, while prayerfully meditating on the
meaning of each mystery.)

The Joyful Mysteries
The Annunciation
The Visitation
The Birth of Jesus

The Presentation
The Finding of Jesus in the Temple

The Sorrowful Mysteries
The Agony in the Garden
The Scourging of Jesus
The Crowning with Thorns
The Carrying of the Cross
The Crucifixion

The Glorious Mysteries
The Resurrection
The Ascension
The Descent of the Holy Spirit
The Assumption of Mary into Heaven
The Coronation of Our Lady

PRAYER OF ST. FRANCIS

O Jesus, through the most pure heart of Mary, I offer you all the prayers, thoughts, works, and sufferings of this day for all the intentions of your divine heart.

Grant, O Lord, that none may love you less this day
    because of me;
that never word or act of mine may turn one soul from you;
and ever daring, yet one other grace would I implore,
that many souls this day, because of me, may love you more.

Lord, make me an instrument of your peace;
    where there is hatred let me sow love,
    where there is injury let me sow pardon,
    where there is doubt let me sow faith,
    where there is despair let me give hope,
    where there is darkness let me give light,
    where there is sadness let me give joy.

O Divine Master, grant that I may
    not try to be comforted but to comfort,
    not try to be understood but to understand,
    not try to be loved but to love.

Because it is in giving that we receive,
it is in forgiving that we are forgiven,
and it is in dying that we are born to eternal life.

PRAYER INVOKING THE PROTECTION OF ST. JOSEPH

To you, O blessed Joseph; we fly in our tribulation and after imploring the help of your most holy spouse, we ask also with confidence for your patronage. By the affection which united you to the Immaculate Virgin, Mother of God, and the paternal love with which you embraced the child Jesus, we beseech you to look kindly upon the inheritance which Jesus Christ acquired by his precious blood, and by your powerful aid to help us in our needs.

Protect, most careful guardian of the holy family, the chosen people of Jesus Christ. Keep us, most loving father, from all pestilence of error and corruption. Be mindful of us, most powerful protector, from your place in heaven, in this warfare with the powers of darkness, and, as you did snatch the child Jesus from danger of death, so now defend the holy church of God from the snares of the enemy and from all adversity. Guard each one of us by your perpetual patronage, so that sustained by your example and help, we may live in holiness, die a holy death, and obtain the ever lasting happiness of heaven. *Amen.*

PRAYER INVOKING ST. MICHAEL THE ARCHANGEL'S AID IN TIME OF SPIRITUAL ATTACK

Holy Michael the archangel, defend us in the day of battle; be our safeguard against the wickedness and snares of the devil. May God rebuke him we humbly pray; and may you, the prince of the heavenly host, by the power of God, thrust down to hell Satan and all wicked spirits who wander through the world for the ruin of souls. *Amen.*

PRAYER FOR A SHARE WITH THE SAINTS

O God our Father, source of all holiness,
the work of your hands is manifest in your saints,

the beauty of your truth is reflected in their faith.
May we, who aspire to have part in their joy,
be filled with the Spirit that blessed their lives,
so that, having shared their faith on earth,
we may also know their peace in your kingdom.

PRAYER FOR THE DEPARTED

Receive, Lord, in tranquility and peace, the souls of your servants
who have departed out of this present life to be with you. Give
them the life that knows no age, the good things that do not pass
away; through Jesus Christ our Lord. **St. Ignatius Loyola**

WAY OF THE CROSS (Modified Family Version)

In the name of the Father. . .

Jesus is condemned to death.
Read Matthew 27:1-2, 11-26. Pause for brief reflection.
We adore you, O Christ, and we praise you.
Because by your holy cross you have redeemed the world.
Our Father. Hail Mary. Glory Be.

Jesus carries the cross.
Read Luke 23:26-27. Pause for brief reflection.
We adore you, O Christ, and we praise you.
Because by your holy cross you have redeemed the world.
Our Father. Hail Mary. Glory Be.

Jesus is nailed to the cross.
Read Mark 15:22-27. Pause for brief reflection.
We adore you, O Christ, and we praise you.
Because by your holy cross you have redeemed the world.
Our Father. Hail Mary. Glory Be.

Jesus dies on the cross.
Read John 19:25-30. Pause for brief reflection.
We adore you, O Christ, and we praise you.
Because by your holy cross you have redeemed the world.
Our Father. Hail Mary. Glory Be.

Jesus is laid in the tomb.

Read Luke 23:50-56. Pause for brief reflection.

We adore you, O Christ, and we praise you.

Because by your holy cross you have redeemed the world.

Our Father. Hail Mary. Glory Be.

Special Introductory Offer

NEW COVENANT

The Magazine of Catholic Renewal

Month by month, *New Covenant* will bring you inspiration, teaching, and personal testimony that will help you:

- deepen your prayer life
- better understand your Catholic faith
- live as a Christian in today's world

Just write to the address below for a free copy of *New Covenant*. If you like what you see, pay the invoice and you'll receive eleven more copies—one year of *New Covenant* for only $14.95.

NEW COVENANT
Department S
P.O. Box 7009
Ann Arbor, MI 48107